T0194670

the beginning
of the end

FRANCE, MAY 1968

◆

ANGELO QUATTROCCHI
and
TOM NAIRN

VERSO

London • New York

This edition published by Verso 1998
© Angelo Quatrocchi and Tom Nairn 1998
First published by Panther Books 1968
© Angelo Quatrocchi and Tom Nairn 1968

All rights reserved

The moral rights of the authors have been asserted

Verso
UK: 6 Meard Street, London W1V 3HR
USA: 180 Varick Street, New York, NY10014-4606

Verso is the imprint of New Left Books

ISBN: 978-1-85984-290-4

British Library Cataloguing in Publication Data
A catalogue record for this book is available from the British Library

Library of Congress Cataloging-in-Publication Data
A catalog record for this book is available from the Library of Congress

Typeset by M Rules, London
Printed by Biddles Ltd, Guildford and King's Lynn

contents

preface

I first read this book when it appeared in the bookshops, some thirty years ago, in the autumn of 1968. Its pages were still warm from the fire of the barricades. It was written while France was in the throes of a general strike involving ten million workers, students and professionals, and while British students were beginning to question and challenge the political system, then presided over by a Labour government under the leadership of Harold Wilson.

The Beginning of the End is a historic document of great value. It is an account of what happened in France in 1968: the first time since the Second World War that a major Western European state appeared to be on the edge of a popular revolution.

The book was the result of a political marriage which brought together two remarkable characters. Angelo Quattrocchi was (and remains) a flamboyant Italian Anarchist of Sicilian ancestry, though he was born and brought up in Como, where his socialist father taught at a local school. Bored by life in Como, Quattrocchi moved to London. Here he mingled in Bohemian and radical circles where he met both Tom Nairn and, more importantly, the young writer and novelist Jill Neville. He fell in love with her. His ever-sensitive antennae alerted him to the potential of Paris. Soon the couple decamped to the Latin Quarter and that is where 1968 found them.

Tom Nairn was a British socialist of Scottish origins. He studied philosophy at Oxford, but his primary interest was aesthetics or, to be more precise, the tradition of the Italian aesthetic philosopher Benedetto Croce. After graduating he went to Pisa, where he had obtained a place at the Scuola Normale to study aesthetics under the direction of Carlo Ragghianti, a pupil of Croce. It was here, through his fellow students, that Nairn encountered the work of Antonio Gramsci (not then translated into English) and through Gramsci discovered Karl Marx. By 1968 he was a Gramscian Marxist who instinctively interpreted politics and society in those terms. This unusual tangent fitted in rather oddly with the main currents of left-wing thought at the time (Lenin, Trotsky, and also Mao Zedong and Che Guevara).

After his return from Italy, Tom Nairn met Perry Anderson and Robin Blackburn through Ralph Miliband. They were engaged in refounding the old *New Left Review*. He introduced his new comrades to the thought of the Sardinian revolutionary. The net result of these discussions was the gestation and birth of the Nairn/Anderson theses on English history, which challenged traditional Marxist assumptions and were to incur the majestic wrath of Edward Thompson: their dialogues represented one of the more celebrated intellectual debates on the British left, whose heights were never to be scaled by epigones of either side.*

The two pieces in this book are different in tone and style, but not in temper. A volcanic passion underlies them both, a passion that

---

*The debate is now being written out of history by some academic historians. Laurence Brockliss and David Eastwood, for example, in one new survey of British history, *A Union of Multiple Identities* (Manchester University Press, 1997), refer to Edward Thompson's 'The Peculiarities of the English' (1978) as the source of the modern historical argument on the nature of the British state (p. 193 and footnote 1, p. 208: 'In a wonderfully suggestive essay Edward Thompson introduced us to the peculiarities of the English . . .'). 'Peculiarities' was republished as a chapter of *The Poverty of Theory and other essays* (London, Merlin Press, 1978). The late Edward Thompson would never have allowed them to get away with such retrospective Stalinism!

expresses hope and optimism for the future. We were all convinced that the French May heralded a new order. This book was written to awaken youth throughout the world, to shake them from their slumber and encourage them to follow their own roads to political and social emancipation.

Quattrocchi's lyrical prose-poem, written on the barricades in Paris and sent in batches to Nairn in London, is the best reportage of the French events of that year. It is a participant's description of the political landscape, written with a fervour that comes only when one lives through big events. It is not something that is easily counterfeited.

Tom Nairn's essay was written during a strike and occupation by the students of Hornsey Art College, where he taught sociology. One of the leaders of that strike, a young Welsh Communist by the name of Kim Howells, is currently a member of the New Labour government, busy transforming dreams into nightmares . . . but I digress.

The burning intelligence of Nairn's essay – wildly optimistic, full of hope, astute and extremely prescient on the nature of the small sects – still shines through after thirty years. Here, too, there is an irony. One of the Trotskyist sects lambasted by Nairn is the French OCI (International Communist Organisation) whose leaders attempted to dissuade students from joining the struggle on the barricades on the night of 10 May. One of the leaders of that organisation was a young militant named Lionel Jospin. I wonder whether, as leader of the French Socialist Party, he appreciated the irony of being propelled into power in 1997 by a wave of strikes by French workers and students who came out on to the streets to defend their welfare state and living standards, reviving memories of that summer in May thirty years ago.

This book is about France, but the irruption of 1968, inspired by the epic resistance of the Vietnamese peasants, was not restricted to Europe alone. It spread throughout the world and affected every continent.* The only immediate success achieved was in Pakistan, where a student

---

*The global impact of 1968 is discussed in *1968: Marching in the Streets* by Tariq Ali and Susan Watkins (London and New York, 1998).

uprising triggered off a more generalised urban revolt and, after four months of continuous struggle and numerous student and worker casualties, toppled the US-backed military dictatorship of Field-Marshal Ayub Khan. Much has changed since then and the collapse of the Soviet Union, accompanied by the restoration of a virulent Mafia capitalism, has transformed the world. It has also, temporarily, pushed Hope aside.

Of the two authors, Angelo Quattrocchi has very much remained a *soixante-huitard*. He lives in Rome and Tuscany leading a traveller's existence. He has written a number of underground guides as well as a popular manual, *How to deal with Children who watch Television*. He has also made two films for Italian television on the politics and culture of the Sixties and Seventies. Life has changed. The world has changed. But Angelo remains the same, a dissident who resists the depradations of an increasingly marketised culture.

His lover of the Sixties, Jill Neville, died in 1997. While Angelo Quattrocchi was sending his reports from the Parisian war zone to London (where they were copy-edited by a young Australian named Carmen Callil for a quick publication by Panther Books), Jill was busy working on a novel, *The Love Germ*, in which Angelo figures as the hero. It, too, has been reprinted by Verso to accompany *The Beginning of the End*. As to which of these two books is the *hors d'œuvre* and which the main course can only be left to the tastes of individual readers. My advice is to read them in tandem.

Tom Nairn's youthful enthusiasm for the ideas of Antonio Gramsci has been deployed to good effect in works such as *The Enchanted Glass*, in which he dissects the English monarchy and its clammy grip on the culture of the United Kingdom. He has subsequently been recognised as one of the leading world authorities on nationalism and the nation state: his latest book on this theme, *Faces of Nationalism*, has also been published by Verso this year.

Re-reading *The Beginning of the End* transported me to the good old days, but a Brechtian dictum reminds us never to start with the good old things, but rather with the bad new ones. I remember well

Tom Nairn's polemical blast at Old Labour in the pages of the *New Left Review*. Long, long ago, when it was deeply unfashionable on the Left to question the lack of democracy in the Labour Party and the trades unions, Nairn referred to the union block vote as 'the dead souls of Labourism'. How one yearns for that withering scorn now as we mark the first year of the New Labour regime. There are many who would like nothing better than for Nairn to turn his attention to the bland culture and politics (not to mention life-politics) that mark the present transition. The grey rules of history, after all, exist only to be broken.

Tariq Ali
London, 1998

foreword

'When the finger points at the moon, the IDIOT looks at the finger. Chinese Proverb.' This was written on a wall of the Paris Conservatoire de Musique, in May 1968.

In the happy month of May, the French performed the first act of their second great Revolution.

This was the first revolution that demanded roses as well as bread, and therefore the greatest of all revolutions, and the last.

Here, we have tried to see the golden moon in the events of May, with a passion worthy of the French people who first broke the grey rules of history in those days, and made it visible.

It cannot be seen with the eyes, only with poetry and the most abstract of thoughts, and these are the two muses invoked here to tell, first of all how, and then why, our pre-history began to end in this place and time.

Our concern is the revolution itself, the meaning victorious among the defeats of May and June, in minds far from Paris. We would like to convince the incredulous, to encourage those daring to hope, and to aggravate the uneasy dreams of those still asleep.

If the grey laws were broken, it is because they have grown old and become breakable. To each according to his imagination. . . .

Angelo Quattrocchi
Tom Nairn

what happened

ANGELO QUATTROCCHI

prelude

This is the tale of the revolution which occurred in Paris in the month of May, 1968.

Revolutions are the ecstasy of history: the moment when social reality and social dream fuse (the act of love).

The reasons given for their happening are always insufficient, their descriptions, always partial.

The May revolution fought for the visible (bread) and the invisible (a new order).

The tale must be told in metaphors.

Need, and consciousness, brought action.

Action against the new order illuminated the carcass of present society. Crystallized the dreams of the 'actor-participants'.

Almost all which is visible has now receded, apparently. The invisible is in people's minds. The minds of the participants.

It has reversed a balance so old as to appear immutable, before this revolution.

The collective hopes of a new order are now incommensurably stronger than the small, private fears nursed by the injustice of the present.

ONE

one pleasure has the bourgeoisie, that of degrading all pleasures

Flashback-Nanterre. A contemporary fable.

1963. Wednesday. Weekly cabinet meeting. A university campus is needed. (*progress*)

Preferably on the outskirts of Paris. (*planning*)

The then Minister of the Army Messmer to the then Minister of Education Fouchet (of the Interior in May '68): 'I have a small piece of land, west of Paris, at Nanterre. You could use that if you want.' (*politics*)

It was an air-force depot, in the middle of wasteland and shantytowns.

Surgit Nanterre.

1968. Concrete and glass; for the middle class of the 16th and 17th arrondissements, the rich residential areas of Paris, her mausoleums. And parking lots; lots of parking lots for the sons of the well to do, who live with the family and use mummy's car. (*the family*)

Around the campus, still the Arab and Portuguese shantytown.

Underdeveloped teenagers playing football (their ribs! their language!) on the periphery of life. Chimneys, council houses, wasteland. On the walls, written by a spray pistol:

URBANITY, CLEANLINESS, SEXUALITY.

Twelve thousand students. Fifteen hundred live in residence.

Dancing once a week, cineclub twice a week, and telly the other nights. Telly, the opium of the masses, but also the self-inflicted masochism of the intellectuals. (*culture*)

On a wall: SQUASH YOUR FACE ON THE WINDOW-PANE LIKE AN INSECT AND ROT.

The rooms are good and sterilized: big glass windows overlooking the Arab barracks. No visits by 'foreigners' allowed, you can't add or change furniture, you cannot cook. No politics on the premises.

On the external walls: HERE FREEDOM STOPS.

Girls (over 21, or with a special parental permission) can visit boys in their rooms. But boys cannot visit girls, because – says the minister – nature has its laws, which are better acknowledged than forgotten. Also – says the minister – 'the girl residents are not really willing to have the boys intrude into their feminine world'. (*ethics*)

A handful of Maoists, trotskyists, anarchists, situationists; yes, and Cohn-Bendit. (*the extremists*)

That is, before the deluge.

Sociology students are the most active. But militants operate in a vacuum. Their only rallying issue: Vietnam. (*mythology of the left, alienation of the majority, consciousness of a few*)

Few names on a black list: the names of the militants. The dean, Grappin, good father, liberal man (he was in the Resistance) denies strenuously the existence of the black list.

But strange raincoated men appear on the campus. They must be the men who check on all 'Vietnam Committees', which are very active in Paris.

The raincoated men take photographs of the 'extremist' students.

The students take photographs of the raincoated men and pin them on the boards.

In the interminable corridors, boards say: 'FLN will win.' And: 'All reactionaries are paper tigers.' Vietnam is in Vietnam. The students ask the sociology professor for Chris Marker's film on the big Rhodiaceta strike to be shown. The professor says no.

The students want to discuss William Reich's books on repression and sexuality. No.

They begin to talk back to the professors.

Who is Charlemagne, professor emeritus?

Charlemagne was a very good king who fought for Christianity.

What do the workers eat for lunch, professor emeritus?

They eat what they get, my children, but let us concern ourselves with the things of the mind, and not be distracted by trivia, because a brilliant future is in store for you, if you apply yourselves with discipline, and learn with discernment.

Anonymous hands write on walls: 'professors, you are old'.

Something is not working, there are cracks in the walls.

Minds are troubled. A few troublemakers excite the students.

Ministers are faintly annoyed.

Minister Missoffe comes to inaugurate the new swimming pool.

He has written a book on youth, as ministers of youth should.

Spotlight. Amphitheatre. Minister speaks, students listen.

Student Cohn-Bendit interrupts: 'I have read your books – he says – Six hundred pages of rubbish, you don't even mention sexual problems.'

Minister in a rage. Loses his cool: 'no wonder – he says – with your face, you have such problems . . . go take a swim in the pool. . . .'

Papers start talking.

The medium being the message, mass media point the road of self-recognition to the students.

The barbed wire of deferential respect is old and rusty. Questions are pincers. The university, factory of knowledge, has its first wildcat strikes.

Professors are kings stripped by questions. Laughter, the gay and suddenly easy art of desecration; professors soon are naked kings.

Under the small-arms fire of the light brigade of vociferous dissenters, joined by the cohorts of the alert and interested, professors run for cover.

News reverberates. Italian students have already learned to cut bus tyres, to throw sand into the eyes of the *flics* pursuing them.

German students are coping with dogs. Civilizations differ from each other. Different answers for different situations.

On the 22nd of March, the students occupy the administrative building singing 'La Carmagnole', especially revised for the circumstance and dedicated to their dean Grappin (*dansons la grappignole . . .*).

Students with frail hands and troubled minds. Students, sons of the bourgeois, enclosed within two ghettos: the university-factory where they give answers but don't ask questions; and the ghetto of privilege.

Their minds are policed by discipline, patrolled by examinations. Their hearts frozen by authority. Their state within the state mimes the society from which they are insulated. And yet, they do not own and they do not belong.

Their past, mystified by the all embracing suffocation of family ties, the humiliating dependence on family money, pushes them towards a present which asserts dogmas and denies learnings; asks for collaboration with the big enterprise of camouflage, collaboration with the perpetuation of production without questions, consumption with no answers.

Their university mimes society, mimes the factory. They threaten its functioning, using gaily and daringly the shreds of learning handed down to them. They reconstruct patiently in the silence of their rooms the pieces of the puzzle which needs them obedient and well behaved, respectful to their grave and grievous masters and mindless to the outside world. And yet the tools they are handed, however blunted by their majestic keepers, spell irreverence and reveal traps, false doors, distorting mirrors, barriers, closed gates. At the very end of the long dusty roads: injustice.

11th April. Rudy Dutschke is shot.

Very fragile ties with those to whom you are similar, who are defying the same small semigods, on the other side of ridiculous frontiers.

In the Latin Quarter students congregate and talk.

Scattered at first, then in groups, finally: a demonstration.

Troubled waters, ripples, waves.

Rotary presses start rolling.

Pierre Juquin, communist M.P., member of the Central Committee of the Communist Party, comes to Nanterre. To talk about the 'communist solution' to the 'student crisis'.

And leaves by the back door.

The 'March 22' constellation attracts the stardust, its brightness illuminates ironically a still very dark sky.

But the university-factory is now in danger. Grains of sand have brought the machine to a grinding halt.

Nanterre, the factory is closed.

The police come, force the students out, line them up, hands behind their necks (Vietcong photos?) and search them for weapons.

Vietnam has never been so far, or so near.

The *flics* do not find weapons.

Tomorrow, the Nanterre students will be at the Sorbonne.

T W O

Thanks to teachers and exams
competitiveness starts at six
(HANDWRITTEN POSTER)

Let's open the gates of nurseries,
universities, and other prisons
(NANTERRE, CONCERT HALL)

Sorbonne the Alma Mater.

Sorbonne mater dolorosa where the dark ancient rites of initiation and consecration are performed. Sorbonne mater dulcissima, where the golden fruits of scholarly minds blossom in secluded cloisters, well protected from the winds of history and the infinite infections of vulgarity. Sorbonne the citadel. Sorbonne the fortress. Dean Roche is a mouse. A pathetic, little, miserable old grey mouse, fond of dusty corners, feeding on the significance of thirteenth century debates about angels on tops of needles.

Dean Roche is also a shit.

In the courtyard of the Sorbonne a few hundred students are discussing politics. Distant politics: Vietnam, and their own politics: the closing of Nanterre.

The police precipitated things there, acting like a catalyst. The students, and some of their teachers-keepers, had to face the emissaries of the naked king, the faceless long-arms of the system which rules by mystification, but when that eventually fails, by brute force.

And as in chemistry, and politics, forces attract or repel, according to your inclination, conscience, interest, understanding, atomic structure, or place in society. Students are economically blackmailed by their families, mentally repressed by the teaching system, but within reach of the tools of understanding.

They are now at the Sorbonne, defiant and very determined, knowing that a squalid commando of thugs nursed by the police might come. (*the Occident*)

Roche, the mouse, is genuinely frightened.

All of his courtyard full of students (he will say on radio).

The minister is uneasy too. The time when an organized band of fascists can cope with student troublemakers is long past.

Roche calls the prefect of police, Grimau, and is assured that the *flics* are ready, in case of an emergency.

Students pack the Latin Quarter.

Roche thinks the situation is beyond control (that courtyard!) and asks Grimau to send his *flics*.

Now, Grimau is a sensible person. Like all people in command he has been a student too (and he also knows what his mercenaries are capable of). He tells Roche he wants the request to be put in writing.

The dean Roche, the mouse Roche and the shit Roche, in one person assembled, signs.

Latin Quarter meeting place, Latin Quarter vicarious myth. Narrow streets of cobblestones.

Boulevard Saint Michel starts at Place Saint Michel, by the river, and goes up, very straight, to the gardens of Luxembourg.

Boulevard Saint Germain crosses it. Place de la Sorbonne is half-way up, on the left.

Place de la Sorbonne is in front of the Sorbonne, which has one entrance there, and another in rue des Écoles. The Sorbonne has a central courtyard. In the courtyard, if one looks up, one sees a square of sky.

Many are the 'species' of *flics* needed for law and order. Metropolitan police: 70 thousand, of which 22 thousand are in Paris. They wear long black raincoats and have batons made of wood, and painted white.

Special intervention groups, the élite of the *flics*, wear khaki uniforms. They are very well trained: specialized in anti-riot techniques.

C.R.S.(S.S.) are a reserve police force, at the disposal of the Minister of Interior. They are fifteen thousand and have black, india-rubber batons.

Les 'gendarmes mobiles' are also in black, they are fifteen thousand strong and take orders from the army. They have rifles.

For practical and poetic purposes, students, demonstrators, and generally the population will soon call them all C.R.S.(S.S.), in a rhythmical, obsessive chant which can be derisory, defiant, mocking, hateful. When referred to in the third person, they will be all called: *flics*. Or, of course, epithets.

Called by Roche, the *flics* surround the Sorbonne, and force their way in from rue des Écoles. The four or five hundred students in the courtyard assemble to one side, near the chapel. Student leaders negotiate with the intruders, and are told that they may leave unmolested, if they leave. By now the *flics* have forced their way in from the other entrance too, and surround the students. The leaders agree to leave, some students are helmeted, some have dismembered two tables and brandish the legs as clubs.

A corridor is formed, a corridor of *flics* through which the students must go out. At the door, they are picked up and thrown into black marias.

Many are roughed up.

Students in adjacent streets see, and pass the word, and shout.

Gatherings. Groups.

Boulevard Saint Michel is students.

Boulevard Saint Germain is students.

Place Saint Michel is packed.

It's five o'clock.

The light artillery of the mass media sends its scouts.

Quivering antennae will rove the arena, indefatigable gnomes of ether will send messages which will trouble all good people in their very private homes.

The state of the battles will be offered in detail, packaged yet murderous, dynamite wrapped in cellophane. In homes where the non-participants hear of the behaviour of their emissaries, blades will penetrate thick layers of consciences.

The young of the frail hands and troubled minds, those evicted from the sleep-castle are only half awake and stirring. From now on they will be in the streets to shout naked words and wishes.

The waves will bring news of their comrades, invisible now through the gases and the rage, to their transistors, useful news, on how the fighting develops from minute to minute.

Gatherings. Groups. The electrons of the atom dance a ballet of self-discovery.

Barrages of black *flics*. Leather and steel and plastic.

Forgotten nightmares. Masks of blindness. Lines of fear.

Sweet and sickening taste in the mouth. Dry palate. Bowels.

Memories of ancient armies, of unbeatable cruel leaders of hordes, unleashing successive waves of screaming furies. Martians. Monsters of planets of steel and ice. Men in uniforms performing dark rites.

Shouts and chanting. Electricity. Lightning. The magic power of the rhythmical word which casts spells. Gatherings around the chants, silver chains of sound, thin protection of air and space.

The first wave.

Scattering butterflies.

The black army is now a wave of black men inflicting pain with white clubs. To be left alone is to be grabbed and clubbed; it is falling down and being kicked by many converging on the prey. A girl lies unconscious. Grenades make bangs and blue clouds.

Radios screech.

Cars circulate: fish in an aquarium.

Cobblestones. Stones found near the trees.

Traffic-signal poles are pulled out. Long spears to attack the black marias and to be used as levers to loosen more cobblestones.

*Pavés.** The streets offer their skin of stones. *Pavés* make arcs which last seconds.

*Cobblestones.

The first *flic* of leather and steel falls, crushingly, his spring broken.
The bangs of the grenades punctuate the battles.

Nauseating gases impregnate streets and lungs. Protection, regrouping, embryos of barricades, then – barricades.

Long files of black marias inexorably working their way up from
Place Saint Michel.

In their receptacles, good people eating their dinners consume the
instant poison from their radios.

Captured students are taken to Notre-Dame-des-Champs police station.

At ten it starts to rain.

At eleven, the flics are masters.

The Sorbonne – ringed in black.

THREE

kiss your love without leaving your gun
(ODEON THEATRE POSTER, OCCUPIED BY THE MAY INSURGENTS)

Rome . . . Berlin . . . Madrid . . .
Warsaw . . . Paris

Captured students are sentenced, by a jury called on the Sunday.

Society is a plastic flower.
The mould is old, fresh sprays of colour are added.
Plastic flowers do not fade. They melt under heat.
Give us this day our daily bread, our monthly bribe.
Shape our dreams and our desires, so that I, and only I can rise.
My office job I will hold tight, my factory job I'll endure with no pride. And when the lonely hours of my survival are over, and I return to my cocoon, my joy, my family will tell me I'm right.
And sweet choruses and grave, will modulate on long waves, the electric communion with my fellow slaves.
The waves have carried disquieting sounds, privileged sons are stirring in their cloisters.
The wall of consensus is showing a crack, only determination can patch it up.
Four students are sentenced, for having been there.
It's Sunday -- the day of prayers.

At night, the *flics* clear all building sites around the Sorbonne of movable material.

The country is fascinated by the kids' folly. The mindless young students are playing with fire.

At six o'clock, Monday morning, three thousand *flics* protect the Sorbonne. The Latin Quarter is patrolled. Water cannons are ready, to cool spirits.

Lightfooted young offspring are flexing their muscles. Being new to the game, they don't seem to fear, being young in their minds, they don't seem to care.

The stage setting is ready.

The students' union and the teachers' union have called a strike.

Unwritten rules, the ones which can be unearthed in cryptograms of balance sheets and profit margins, silently and categorically state, that rebellious workers must be faced by the army, and shot at. Agitating students are best dealt with by clubs and tear-gas.

A threat is a threat, a nuisance is a nuisance.

And the ruling society mustn't be caught in the act of murdering its own children. The consequent outcry would be more disrupting than the actual disturbance.

By nine o'clock the Latin Quarter is virtually sealed off with peasants made watchdogs and clad in Martian plastic. They wear gloves over hands rescued from the obscure pains of the spade.

But hundreds of students have already infiltrated the enemy's lines. Their knowledge of the terrain is an asset.

The *flics* cannot but keep to the crossroads, and their maps. Cohen-Bendit and others present themselves at the door of the Sorbonne. A disciplinary committee is ready for them inside.

They enter singing the International. To the *flics* they had told how exploited they are.

A chorus of students chant the C.R.S.(S.S.) litany.

The C.R.S.(S.S.), true to their profession, and also their inclination, as events will show, launch the attack.

Screaming and tear-gas and beatings and sirens and wounded again.

The incongruous ballet.

Now grenades are shot by guns, not in an arc, but straight at the demonstrators, meant to maim.

The battle spreads. The students, on foot, are highly mobile. The *flics*, who do not dare to go so far from their cars for fear of getting lost in a hostile environment, are pinned down. Monstrous car jams. The *flics* are stuck by the neutral traffic. Rudiments of urban guerriglia. The kids disappear in thin air. A helicopter appears over the Latin Quarter. Regrouping is easy and heartening. Then, the crossing of the river, geographical escalation.

Marching and singing in the streets of collective euphoria.

The day is bright as the march takes to a brisk exhilarating hop hop invented by Japanese colleagues.

The thousand chant that they are just 'groupuscules', streaming down avenue de l'Opéra rather astonished.

Humanité and *Figaro* are convinced that it is the doing of 'extremist groups'. Malefic influences.

Hopping back home. To the magic Quarter. In gymshoes.

Fed by sandwiches and excitement.

Radios are duly recording for the citizens.

Through Saint Germain to Maubert Mutualité. The black barrage is there. Still life. Human cordon to prevent contact with blackness.

The *flics* charge. By surprise.

Scattering and shuffling and running away. Many of them are caught, and lie now on the pavement. The price to pay for joy. Scarlet and black.

A few hundred yards lost to the S.S.

Madness, anger, fury, rage. Frustration.

Cars are put across and barricades made and the counter-attack is a cauldron of folly.

Running towards the blackness with *pavés* or with nothing but outrage. Running towards barriers of tear-gas till you fall, suffocated. A red rag in your hands. Or a black one.

A hut catches fire. The *flics* charge again and again now.

The students hold their ground. Radio reporters shout in microphones which reach very far, into office catacombs, into home fortresses.

This is rioting. The ballet is Grand Guignol.

F O U R

dessous les pavés la plage

Grimau, prefect of police, a reasonable man, comes to Maubert to see the incredible. People are leaving their offices.

A middle-aged man, crossing the square on the quiet side, is attacked by a black uniformed man who smashes his head. Others run. He is clubbed madly and then kicked. An officer comes and tears them away from the body.

Grimau is brought to the radio-car. He says in the microphone that 'a *flic* is always a *flic*'. 'A helmet to protect himself. A club to defend himself.'

He was a student too, and has been clubbed himself.

Students say into the microphone that the *flics* are assassins.

The arena is an ever-growing bubble, sucking in all that is young against all that is black.

Small vibrating waves infiltrate nudgingly the silence outside. The silence continuously badgered by the voices of the exemplary confrontation. It is scaringly and irremediably miming something else. The blind millions at the receiving end lose consistence. Apartment walls are getting thinner. Screens are torn. Water cannons are used in Saint Germain to disperse groups.

A man in a bow tie is hit and rolls over the pavement.

The bubble is now all tear-gas. Students are assembling at Denfert Rochereau (Montparnasse) for the demonstration called by their union and the teachers' union. Professors (apart from the emeriti in their dark niches) are reassessing their morals and bringing them up to date.

Clubs cracking on skulls hammer into their heads the immemorial defeats of the classrooms. The *consecutio temporum* is being gassed. The men of evil are finishing a job they never started.

One of the screens changes side, in the name of humanity, learning, and all its corollaries. At heart, many of them are only hostages, conscious and split. Teaching is a dangerous trade.

The precious sandcastle supported daily by their saliva is falling.

Teenagers, the high school kids sweating absurdities in their Lycée reformatories are in rebellion. They are eighteen, they are fifteen, they are younger, they are the age of the cardboard heroes of a dusty yellowish book. The age of Helen of Troy, the age of Patroculus killed by the skill of Hector, father and leader, the age of myth that myths cannot destroy. Ruthless and gay, tied by bonds of respect and carefully guarded. Pullovers and jeans will claim the streets, mocking savagely empty idols, powerful yesterday. From classrooms which mock learning and teach absurdity. From the schools where you are taught to be sheep, where you learn to bleat dates of bloody battles and idiot tales of murderous generals.

Out to Denfert to shout their approval of blessed desecration which has them unmasked, out into the squares for the right to learn right and the right to be wrong. To face tear-gas which makes you vomit. Out there where comrades are massacred for a change of textbooks, where resignation is spelled in so many pages it's almost acceptable.

They are thousands and thousands in Denfert and Saint Germain is still fighting.

SHOUT – says a wall and the bubble is bursting.

The fetish of the elders, cars, are used as lovely barricades stopping the black troops who smash through thick gas and beat the wounded; hate on commission and hurt with impunity.

They scream when unleashed, releasing their fear of what they do not know and do not understand.

They are trained to despise and paid to be hated.

They are stronger and armed, they are the masks of repression, yet they are human and miserable, and scared when confronted.

They fight for their shilling, we fight for ideas.

Bodies are picked up and put on stretchers which soon are made bloody by constant use. The crying goes high into a sky which cannot be seen by eyes full of tears from the exploding grenades.

And dawn brings more fighting and the two water cannon trucks ready into position but vulnerable to the bravest *pavés* which shatter the windscreen and make them retreat. It slowly gets quieter, exhaustion takes over, the *flics* are masters of a dark Latin Quarter, watching the corners, fearful of shadows, but ready to maim and hurt the isolated and beat the unaware and scare the 'civilians' who are just passing there.

The shattered battalions of students and schoolkids have now retired in order to rest. And to tell their friends they must all help because confrontation is becoming insurrection and it's clear to everyone what *they* stand for and what they are facing in order to get it.

It's an uneasy evening for telly watchers in spite of the fact that they see nothing because the *officiators* are there to lull.

But radios are busy sending out signals. Radios which thirst for shows to offer to the hungry masses: truth is sometimes helped by free enterprise, small thanks for that.

The government says it's the doing of some extremists, and it's time for dialogue, constructive dialogue.

The communists specify that it's trotskyists and anarchists and suchlike troublemakers. They have been seen recently at factory gates trying to talk to the workers about bread and the state of affairs. They are sons of the bourgeoisie and therefore dangerous. But all the same the C.P. condemns repression and police brutality, which can only threaten the peace of the people and stir feelings which are better left quiet so that progress can progress and studious students do their work.

F I V E

be a realist, demand the impossible
(CENSIER)

Now it's beginning to look as if it's cracking.

Between the sheets of their own quiet beds, the parties are stirring.

Telephone calls made by the corporals tell the Union Headquarters that the workers are waking.

The sons of the rich might have fancy dreams, but police repression means only one thing. Young kids with their minds can do what they want, but if it's come to the slaughter, there must be a good reason. Trouble is, the kids might have started for fun, out of boredom or madness, but they are saying they are determined, and fighting to death. If they were there for nothing, it would soon be over.

Students and teachers are again at Denfert. They say: 'down with repression' and march again.

In the dusk, many faces are white. It's the talcum powder on their faces, against the gas. Many wear handkerchiefs covering their mouths and noses, drenched in lemon juice, against the gas. Some wear goggles. They march briskly because it's cold this evening, and as long as the *flics* stay away, they'll keep warm by singing the International.

Archangels of many 'isms', armed with the polished and blunt tools of their ideologies. Sects which with religious education have devoted their lives to the Word. And were mostly ignored.

But then at Nanterre among the ashes of the past revolutions they struck a few coals still warm. Dissent and desecration became tentative theories, a permanent violation of codes their tactic. And the incredibly simple little core of truth, buried under geological strata slowly sedimented, came to the surface.

Contempt was their daily bread and tool. Contempt for the absurdity of the university-factory and the university-temple sharpened the words which cut through the seven thousand veils. And the words became actions. Then (and only then), others rallied, incredulous and shy, misty-eyed and enthusiastic.

It was an easy journey. Authority crumbled under the barrage of outrageous questions and in came the *flics*.

And the vestals of small carefully arranged altars turned their backs on their shrines and joined each other in the pursuit of the wounded monster. The '22nd March' with light and terrible logic, proclaimed the hunting season open. The sound of the horns was irresistible.

The stream is becoming a river.

The march has to avoid the Latin Quarter this time and so it goes to the right bank and grows steadily.

The inevitable law of gravity attracts bodies. Past decades of Ptolemaic thoughts are stripped to their essentials: red and black flags now held with naïvety and simple determination. And the Ptolemaic system of the unmovable seven skies swears to its Gods that the stars are fixed in a crystal firmament, the earth at its centre. But the very skies are moving. There will be still more fighting tonight, in the Latin Quarter, for the law is simple. Force has only brute force, and its reason of existence determines its nature, which is vile and low.

The purpose of the enemy is to break your bones, the only target he can see. Your purpose is to defend the collective imagination now gathering momentum. The enemy has to strike and necessarily does. Two cafés are besieged and filled with gas. Unmentionable acts of savagery are committed late at night on isolated people and small groups.

Do not wear any red, if alone. Because the long nights of terror have started. The nights of the witchhunt.

And as day follows night, the movement feeds itself.

In Lille and Lyon they are marching too, and in Toulouse, and Marseille. Strasbourg is not quiet. Ministers talk of tolerance.

At Rennes, the students are marching with the unemployed. . . .

S I X

Those who make a revolution by halves,
dig their own graves
(SORBONNE COURTYARD, NEAR THE CHAPEL, AND ELSEWHERE)

A Philistine's tears are the
nectar of the Gods

When attacked, the movement bleeds and gains momentum, when left alone it gains friends and sympathy.

The archangels send messages to the factories. To the factories where the prime injustice is perpetrated, where the oppression is tangible.

The source of the original sin of Capital, the paradigm of the other spheres.

Where they produce in blindness according to the alien laws of masters so powerful that they are invisible.

There where no question may be asked, if bread is to be gained, where the bread is meagre and the machines are heavy, where the slaves of the machines are given hell inside to earn their purgatory outside . . .

They have unions, preaching a revolution that their offspring will maybe see and a resignation rewarded by crumbs falling from the resplendent and implacable table. They are skilled at bargaining for crumbs, the unions. Armed with solid minds and textbooks, their officials know that life is misery, but production has its laws. They heal the wounds and guard the fire. They are convinced that the share will get bigger and anyway workers are afraid for their jobs,

and they have families and now want a car, so one by one they are
afraid of a past poverty still visible because many don't work.

Living examples that it can get worse and therefore they know that
the workers taken one by one only want money, another little bit
which is difficult to get, it must be snatched, and that's why they are
there in the first place, till the time will come when the other classes
will get a bit softer and vote to the left so we make a left government
which will make more houses and more little cars to be given to the
workers and they'll feel better just like the other classes and everything
will be better because the party will decide all the nice good things that
the country needs, so stick to the union and vote for your party and if
it's not this decade it might be the next. We will take over the industries
then and run them better but for now you've got to wait and join the
unions and come on strike when called and let them see you're there.

The unions are worried, they are for law and order and this student
unrest looks too much like an uprising.

If the show doesn't end they may have to show solidarity, it looks
very dangerous. Minds get confused and there are the young workers
in factories too, they are the most exploited; they have good reflexes
which burn out in a few years but are good for production. They are
very unruly and often disrespectful.

Séguy and Descamps, leaders of the C.G.T. (communist) and
C.F.D.T. (catholic left) meet student leaders. In order to show our
understanding and support for students and teachers and all workers
of the mind whom we call intellectuals and who are very important in
the scheme of things and want just more freedom in their own universities and who are now confronted by brutal repression of the
reactionary forces we think it's advisable to organize a demonstration in
which our troops will show their numbers and in so doing convince
the government that reform must be met since the times are changing.

The country is now listening intently to the avalanche-roar of all
these young people marching and fighting.

They want the Sorbonne, and their comrades out of prison.

They want the *flics* out and they want other things which can be imagined when they shout assassins to the *flics* beating them.

The government doesn't know if it's better to open the Sorbonne and take away the *flics* or to continue the beating which is sharpening the conscience of those listening to their radios, frankly disgusted. But the dilemma is painful. Events have shown that even when not attacked they still grow in numbers and even the most timid as we all know have some grievances.

But the main argument is that grievance is omnipresent, and power must not be seen to give in to determined action, otherwise the principle of authority is shaken.

And history teaches that it's exactly at that moment that a rebellion becomes revolution.

The Sorbonne remains closed.

S E V E N

I take my desires for reality,
because I believe in the reality of my desires
(SORBONNE, AMPHITHEATRE, AND ELSEWHERE)

Action = not reaction – but creation
(CENSIER)

Days and nights run into each other in a continuous flow of events made by the young militants and their friends and echoes of the thunder now cover all other sounds. The sounds of silence and daily cares, the infinite little noises of small lives and small fears.

Many are listening, some are unquiet, some obscurely afraid, because the signs are there.

'Commodities are the opium of the people.'

Written over a wall of the National Popular Bank, and quickly effaced by its valets.

'They are buying your happiness. Steal it,' is still there on a wall.

In the apparent calm of the buses, between the silent deserts of underground journeys, under the immense plastic vault of the media suddenly reflecting the lightning of mock and cruel battles, snakes of doubt are appearing. The eternal populace of working-class districts, used to painful survival and their own hard-earned mockery of the state of their betters, feels the scorn inflicted by these rebellious sons.

The youngest, squashed between the sweet and sour and humiliating tyranny of the bourgeois family and the pompous absurdity of their Lycée barracks, are now rampant in the streets, the first to mock, the last to retreat.

There is a taste of revenge for a struggling people who count their pennies in this sudden explosion.

The wild flowers who have gathered up the flags of their fathers' ancient battles and are claiming the right to be called 'comrade' and are fighting like tigers in a sea of gas for the honour of their minds and the courage of their dreams.

In other fights buried deep in books which they cannot read, the poor have always been joined by the best of the privileged.

But now these kids, the vanguard of the future, are carving alone a space for their dreams and crying to the sky that the rich are also slaves of the injustice they preserve. That the arrogance and glory of their houses and their gardens masks the emptiness and the darkness filled by rituals and stupidity.

Young workers and the young left to rot in the meaninglessness of the ghettos have heard the distant clamour of the theatrical battles.

Some have joined in bringing with them the nihilism of those with no hope to the battle of dreams that their opposites are waging (*blousons noirs*).

The archangels are screaming with desperate voices that the workers should join and then they'll be unbeatable.

And Friday comes and they are all there, they are thousands and thousands and the youngest are glowing. It's days since they have eaten, it's nights since they have slept.

Even the medical students in their white coats, the most apolitical, who care only for the flesh, even they have come. Is it because of the splintered skulls they have patched, the sawing they have done? (I have seen kids queuing quietly to be treated by a white-coated student in the midst of a battle and then returning to their own front line . . .)

And they march towards the Magic Quarter, once again. Towards the Sorbonne, grim with *flics*, an empty shell where Roche the mouse is now master of his walls and mustiness.

And happiness streams towards the Quarter, ignoring the black fences: immobile statues of horror. But when the head has reached the top of Saint Michel, the joy of being back and not molested; the joy of being there and all in one piece becomes determination.

Halt!

Comrades! A decision for 30 thousand.

The *flics* are stone. They watch and wait.

Shut in an office, ministers taste impotence.

Comrades. We dig in and stay. Dawn is coming rapidly.

The *flics* await a telephone call and fret. We dig in and stay, stay till the *flics* go away. As simple as that.

It's dark now and the barricades mount in rue Gay-Lussac. It's dark and in rue Saint Jacques they have already put up the red and black flags. It's dark and the May Commune is born.

Tender hands make chains and pass the *pavés*. And one *pavé* and another makes a rebellion and another one makes a revolution and another one makes the Commune.

Chanting. Songs reverberate from street to street.

Delirium can be touched like water.

It's ten o'clock on the transistors.

Roche the mouse, from inside the lonely walls, squeaks. His masters have ordered him to negotiate. The radios offer their services. Old women throw chocolate bars from windows. The Commune is hungry. The end products of production put to the edification of the collective dream. Cars are good for barricades. Private cars to build public happiness.

A man comes down from his flat himself to push his car towards a barricade. The Commune fortifies itself. In an office, ministers consult.

Transistors have been put on the window-sills. The insurgents are busy, transfigured. People descend from their apartments and help.

The students want the *flics* out, the Sorbonne and their imprisoned comrades freed.

At the Ministry of Interior, Joxe, interim Prime Minister, Fouchet, big chief of the *flics*, Tricot, de Gaulle's left hand and Grimau, the Prefect of Police. They fear that tomorrow Paris will wake up to barricades.

Barricades are spreading, while Cohn-Bendit goes to talk to the mouse. But he is already left behind.

The Commune spreads.

The mouse squeaks: 'Reason can still prevail. The Paris Dean and his colleagues ask the students to abandon the atrocious conflict they are engaged in.' The strident voice brings revulsion, and chill.

The Commune is feverish.

The living-rooms are breathless.

Time waits now, still and heavy. Negotiations are over.

In the office, Grimau, the man of arms, is lucid. The ministers are only puppets, but Grimau sees the insurrection spreading. The population is with them. The stupid radios are offering to the population at large a mirror in which they can see their consciences. In Paris, in the provinces, in the villages. The actors are coming out on to the stage and invite the sheepish audience to join in. It catches quickly. There are workers with them too.

If the barricades are left to stand till dawn, the impossible is at hand.

The ministers are scared. De Gaulle sleeps. (Has a telephone call been made?)

Grimau wins the day.

So, once again, it's massacre.

The Commune is at peace till 2.16 in the morning.

Then: hell.

E I G H T

The May Commune
(RED PAINT ON A WALL OF THE COMMUNE)

La société est une fleur carnivore
(ON A WALL OF THE COMMUNE)

There is logic in their folly
(AFTER SHAKESPEARE: NANTERRE, THIRD LANDING)

Who shall sing the night of the Commune?
  The black sea charges in rue Gay-Lussac. The guns shoot cascades of grenades. The first barricade bursts into flames. The black waves exhale blue gases, the gases are low and pestiferous, the air is blue thickness.
  Acid is yellow.
  Flares are red. Fires crackle. Shots deafen. Shots, and deluge.
  Paris, lend your ears and hear the screaming of your troops advancing. Hear the shouting of your masked men running through their gases and shooting at your kids, your hopes, your tenderness, your reason.
  Blackness advances in a halo of fire.
  The air is blue: thickness.
  Acid is yellow. Flames burst and devour. The first position untenable.
  'Don't panic comrades – they can only take our lives – get away before you faint – don't get in the way of those throwing *pavés*. . . .'
  One barricade. Behind, another. Between them: bodies.

'Don't leave your friends behind, comrades.'

The next barricade.

Dry lungs and tears and blood.

Behind closed doors Paris waits for murder to be done, so its cars can circulate again.

In Saint Michel the first barricade is on fire. A red flag is burning. In Gay Lussac hell is advancing slowly.

People throw water from windows, broken water pipes flood the streets, people scream from windows, shout frightened obscenities at the advancing live tentacles. *Flics* shoot grenades through windows.

Do not stay behind, nobody stays behind when we abandon a barricade.

Crying, between the shots.

The adolescent girl not allowed out after eleven is a bloodstained pullover lit by barricades in flame.

In rue Lacépède a wall says, in white paint: 'It's bleeding.' And if it bleeds, cry SS to the slaves who have learned to hate for a shilling, shout to the closed and respectable houses of Paris that the people indoors are dead, they cannot be living.

The gas makes you cry, burns the lungs, provokes nausea and suffocates.

Duck in time. Run when necessary.

The barricades in Gay-Lussac must be kept as long as possible, the front must be kept, encirclement must be prevented. There will always be time to escape through Place de la Contrescarpe.

Rue d'Ulm is fighting now, Gay-Lussac still holds, Marie Curie is a hospital.

The *flics* try to break in. Screaming hordes. They beat the wounded, take them from the stretchers and beat them.

Monod is there, a Nobel prize professor who is still learning with his pupils. Reporters scream the horror into the transistors.

Colder men in manipulating rooms insist that they calm down or switch their voices off. They break with music.

It's fighting in rue de l'Estrapade now and Saint Michel burns like a torch. The Commune is losing yards, inch by inch, blocks, barricade by barricade. The carnage is about to begin.

Monod is *almost* calmly appealing to the people to come and prevent the massacre before he is switched off. To slow down the attackers, in small streets, put two cars across to make a V, a third one to make a Y, if there is time, and set them on fire.

Keeping the last barricades is essential, commandos take turns at the front line, and last till suffocation. Then others take their places. Remember, the *flics* are vile but not good fighters, because they are mercenaries. Ambulances cannot get through and the white-coated doctors and nurses are beaten. The Commune's hospitals and first-aid units need penicillin, scalpels, oxygen, cotton wool and doctors.

The Commune is bleeding.

A doctor is blocked with a girl who has been blinded, trapped by the *flics*. He implores a reporter to use the radio to tell the chief of *flics* to tell his *flics* to let him get through.

Good samaritans come to collect the pieces, taximen come and snatch the wounded from the *flics*. *Flics* are seen beating those bringing drugs and pulverising the drugs. . . .

Fighting is fierce on the last streets of the Commune. Gas is blue, acid is yellow, the barricades burst into flame.

And kids don't leave them. They fight through the flames, through the splattered blood and the mud, and through the *flics doing things unspeakable*.

Everyone can see that the May Commune has almost lost its territory, and yet is winning.

And when the last of the barricades is untenable, when fear of being surrounded is as tangible as the sirens screaming their bloody victory and closing the ring, dawn is almost there.

Terror is not a word. Terror is the enemy pursuing the fugitives into the courtyards. Terror is running up unknown stairs and banging on closed doors which do not open. Terror is hiding in recesses and hearing the sirens getting nearer.

It's cold, it's cold in the morning and the street resounds, it's bitter cold and the Commune has been murdered.

Feet running, murmurs and doors opened quickly and quietly. Long screams in courtyards, frightened kids suddenly in tears and running.

Silhouettes in corners and niches, hiding, dark on dark.

Cohn-Bendit wants a radio, wants to ask those who are still letting themselves be massacred to get out of the area. Very small crowds still linger. Now it's only beating and beating and beating, please get out and run away, please get away, we need you, don't get caught. Some doors are ajar, some will be forced open by the enemy who is now master. De Gaulle is getting up. The Commune is dead.

Near Place de la Contrescarpe, its last stronghold, a hand has written, in enormous letters now bathed by fire-light:

'Society is a carnivorous flower.'

In the beauty and folly of the night, another hand had written:

'Amongst the *pavés*, I come alive.'

But day follows night. Cohn-Bendit had asked, in a broken voice, for all the forces of the left, for all the unions, for all the parties, for all the people, for the whole population whose conscience was for one night held within a small box full of noises, to upsurge.

The Commune, a flower, like a flower crushable, like a flower ephemeral, has lost its territory, and gained its future.

The powerful leaders of the masses, the cold vestals of the ashes of a revolution always beyond the horizon, wake up early.

By 7 o'clock Waldeck Rochet feels ready to condemn, to lend solidarity, to give his party's support.

Parties and unions come to agreements.

Young blood goes further than old ideals.

On Monday: general strike all over the country. A mass demonstration in Paris. The whole left will be there.

General rejoicing and flags.

NINE

When the General Assembly becomes a
bourgeois theatre, bourgeois theatres
must become the General Assembly
(THE FREE ODEON)

Pompidou the Prime Minister, ex-professor of Latin and Greek in a Marseille Lycée, comes back from Afghanistan, and tries the other method. The Sorbonne will be given back to the students.

Much too late.

The chess game has begun.

The parties of the left and the unions are now in agreement. They will demonstrate, calmly and in an orderly fashion, through the streets of Paris, just as they do on the first of May. Only this time it will be exceptional, because it will be against 'police repression'.

At Beaujon, the *flics'* concentration camp, bloodstained students trickle out into the 'normal' world.

Unions and parties agree to march through the Latin Quarter.

Very quietly, the kids have occupied the science faculty, and the faculty of letters at Censier.

The government is counting on the communists to 'keep the demonstration calm and orderly'.

And the general strike too.

Marches also in all the big towns, in most of the smaller ones and in some of the villages.

The *stage* happening has ended in nightmare. The sound-waves must have brought shame to the honest, bewilderment to the blind, and pure white rage to the understanding. Like a long undulatory earthquake the shockwaves have shaken the crust, though nothing is visible. The country now lives through images. A few ostriches ignore them, buried in their own emptiness.

And there they all come, in broad daylight, under a blue Paris sky kept for the best Mayday occasions.

Unions and parties start at Place de la République, the young at Gare de l'Est.

Action destroys faction.

By early afternoon, the two crowds have become one, the space in between filled by people.

The young fought for a future, against the present, and have resurrected a glorious past.

But it is a million-people Kermesse, and a ceremony.

The last red mass attended by the population.

The 'people' in the streets, the bourgeois at the windows.

A rite once performed in defiance, now re-enacted in self-satisfaction.

The clerics are there, arm-in-arm in dignified parade.

The party men, the union men and, third, the intellectuals.

And yet the procession is impressive, as processions are. More.

Because the unpredictable is at hand. Telephone calls tell that in factories and working-class districts the cohorts are intractable, often rebellious.

All the faithful watchdogs, the Stalinists of proven faith, will be now brought in, and they are there.

Because a million people cannot be fought by the *flics*. And a million people could very easily take over public buildings. A prostrate ghost government couldn't very well give the order to shoot a million people and that is clear to many and that is why the communists and the unions play police to their own people, when very pacifically they could really take over.

When boulevard Saint Michel is reached students' loudspeakers ask everyone to march in silence, for the comrades wounded in street-fighting and beaten in police stations. Silence falls.

The procession ends at Denfert Rochereau – where the young started their marches the old will end theirs. Kids' smiles are bitter. At Denfert, the stupid stone lion sits in the middle of the square.

The stewards, self-appointed police, are thousands strong, and grimly determined.

At Denfert, their loudspeakers, in tones which rise from bonhomie to chilliness, ask the comrades to disperse towards boulevard Arago, towards nothingness, in 'calm, order and dignity'.

A strong human C.P. cordon channels them very efficiently. The other side of the square, on the other side of the cordon, are the students and the young. A loudspeaker is heard with difficulty to say: 'those who want, go back to your tellies . . . students, young workers, down towards boulevard Raspail . . .'

A gigantic strainer with innumerable small holes. (We cut through the flow and cross the cordon almost defiantly, we meet friends at the other side as if by magic . . .)

Down to the Champs de Mars, a park by the Tour Eiffel. A rectangular green space where the assembly of the free and the fighting is constituted.

Behind, Denfert is still emptying.

The militants talk now to a sitting crowd, talk of the procession that has been, and of the fighting which is to come.

The sky is purple.

And when it's darker, as in assemblies of free men, one course of action becomes evident.

'À la Sorbonne!'

The *flics* are hidden under the Iéna bridge, motionless. They had been taken away from the Latin Quarter and the Sorbonne the night before the demonstration, they couldn't have been left there, could they?

So the students have won their citadels, the parties and unions have made their show and retained their troops, and the ghost government has saved its skin.

In the rest of the country, many police headquarters have been besieged by militants. Population, workers and students were closer. In almost all instances, the police stayed away. In many places, it barricaded itself in the police headquarters.

The strike, the figures say, is satisfactory. It has been called by the unions, and it has only been 'satisfactory'. This must be remembered.

TEN

Alma mater. Mater dulcissima,
mater amatissima, mater nostra

Sorbonne. Alma Mater. Sorbonne: mater dulcissima, mater amatissima, mater nostra.

VIOLATE YOUR ALMA MATER.

The flags are two. The red, to scare the bourgeoisie. The black to scare the apprentice bourgeois, their alter egos – the communist with a party card in his pocket and a sergeant's star over his heart.

Communist Catala explains why the parties and unions dispersed at Denfert: 'It was decided by the sponsoring committees . . . which had not sanctioned any further developments . . .'

Catala is the secretary of the Communist Student Union.

'With a million people, almost anything is possible' says Cohn-Bendit – 'On the day of the revolution, you'll tell us to forego it because it hasn't been sanctioned by the appropriate sponsoring committee . . .'

The audience of the big amphitheatre explodes.

Exactly – comrade, exactly.

In other halls, in long corridors leading to halls and other corridors, in the courtyards once silent, up the staircases leading to the upper floors and other corridors, and other rooms: people.

The Sorbonne, once grey, once cold, seven centuries old.

The people, fresh and tired from the action of the streets and the mind. Rather uncomfortable within their own skin and bursting to speak.

They start writing furiously on neutral walls.

'Power to the imagination.'

Imagination is taking power.

Escalating over the horizons and reporting back to mortals.

White paint, red paint, black paint. Paint.

Stones in ponds, gentle ripples.

'I take my desires for reality, for I believe in the reality of my desires': Anonymous. 1968. (1905–1917–1936 . . . remember Mayakovsky?)

De Gaulle is leaving this evening for Bucharest, where he has friends in high places.

A galaxy of poets. The vertigo distillates its words.

Arrows lost in the sky.

'Art is dead, don't eat its corpse.'

Revolution is the ecstasy of history.

'Those who make a revolution by halves, dig their own graves.'

The mystifications are very old:

'How can one think freely in the shadow of a steeple.'

And very new.

'Commodities are the opium of the people.'

Near the main entrance, the edict of the May Commune: 'To forbid is forbidden.' May 1968.

More people. The thirst for physical communion equals the thirst for expression.

In the beginning was the word, then came the means of distant communication manipulated by crystal hands, and people become shadows of themselves. Reflections of amorphous images floating in a space, which is neither here nor now. . . .

Subtle catechisms of words and music, disembodied and ever-present, soothing, obsessive, murmuring soft lies, filling time, filling minds. . . .

'Let's be cruel' – says a wall.

'Humanity will be happy when the last capitalist is strangled with the guts of the last bureaucrat' – another answers.

At the entrance of the amphitheatre, on the pillar by the right, already the epitaph:

'Run forward, comrade, the old world is behind you.'

The night recedes tonight to unlit corners, where shapes rest, oblivious to motions and commotions.

Those last to see fervour in the transfigured faces of their new companions.

A grand piano plays Chopin in the courtyard, by the chapel. Dawn is coming, by a different route.

By mid-morning, the grand piano is playing jazz and de Gaulle is in Rumania.

At the General Assembly, the Prime Minister talks of co-operation.

Strasbourg University declares itself free and autonomous.

Paris is a cauldron.

The Sorbonne is a navel.

The parties of the left call for a motion of censure.

'When the General Assembly becomes a place for idle talking, all places of talk become the general assembly.' Wall writing.

On Wednesday evening, frustrated intellectuals and sympathizers will take over the Odéon Theatre, put up a black and red flag, and proclaim free entry to the students and workers. Many bourgeois will come to this place of instant discussion and public confessions. Theatre is the audience. An obvious popular success, very feeble stylistically, with occasional flashes of greatness.

The thirst for talk finds its water.

E L E V E N

Those who haven't any power to determine
their life, those are the workers
(CENSIER)

Who built Thebes of the seven gates?
The books record only kings' names.
But did the kings dig up the boulders?
. . . . .
Imperial Rome is full of arches.
Who built them?
. . . .
So many reports
So many questions
(B. BRECHT)

The students have taken over the universities.

The workers can take over the factories.

Not that simple.

The umbilical cord the archangels have established between the students and the young workers is fragile, almost nothing, a spider's
thread shining through the foliage of forest now lit by the sun, but a
brisk gesture can break it.

The unions are strong. Entrenched in the workers' camp which they
have occupied for decades.

They are there to alleviate the misery of the working condition, to
bargain for the always meagre bread. And just recently, they have

started to talk of butter; butter too, the unions can get, and nobody can be despised for wanting a bit of butter, if the meal is meagre. And they also promise, in a long distant future which wanes between the sky and the horizon, a time when the workers will be *much better* off because they'll take the government and make things for us, and not just for the bourgeois.

Bread for now, and a mythical future for those who need myths. The unions are strong, and the party is behind them. The party is there to take care of the future.

And yet the unions are weak, very weak. Because most workers don't see much point in joining unions like that, and some do not care or are afraid, especially there where those who belong to the unions are always in danger of being sacked. Which proves that the unions can't really do much.

And the three million foreign workers are scared of losing their jobs, or of being thrown out of the country, they don't speak the language. There is sometimes bad feeling because they take on jobs which our kind could take.

Some workers think (not many) that the unions certainly do not do much for them. They are the pariahs.

So, only one worker in five belongs to a union. Most to the C.G.T. (communist) and half that number to the C.F.D.T. (catholic left).

So the unions are strong, but also weak.

They are weakest where it counts: young workers don't like them much. They call for strikes to order. A few hours one day for a few pennies the next. When the workers explode, because the rhythms are untenable and the money miserable and life unendurable or the little bosses bastards, more often than not the unions cool their men, play chess, use influence, softpedal, sometimes they threaten.

Young workers don't like the unions much.

And the unions are scared of young workers, who often explode and don't care, because they are not so afraid of losing their jobs, one job is like another, and if there isn't any it's just too bad and you can only take so much, in a factory where you are watched all the time like a criminal.

Above all, unions hate wildcat strikes. Strikes which start like a fire, and it's always young people.

The union members are mostly not young. They have gone through the strikes, they have gone through the years in the factory and learned that one has to join, even if sometimes it's not easy, but one joins because the workers need an organization, to protect them day by day and to organize them when the strikes come (when?). He knows it's difficult to bring all of them out on strike, and there is always the few who side with the bosses . . . and unity is necessary to make the pickets, because they are always ready to send the *flics* after a few black-legs, and those who are afraid might follow, and there, you have lost and the union officials don't even get to talking with the bosses, and the union man eats dirt when he goes back, if he is not sacked for having been too active. The party? Now the party has its role to play to get wider support from the other classes, so it will be stronger at elections and change things at the roots (at the top?).

But the party seems to have lost its fire, with all this playing for all these years. And then there is Russia where socialism is made, and it doesn't seem such a paradise but there's no more injustice, and anyway the workers get their full share (full? share?) . . . The union men are hardened by their lives in the factory. Doubts are there but life goes on. And they are tired after working and want to go fishing, or play cards and drink a few glasses at the local. The unions and the party are strong, but they are also very weak. Their best people sometimes leave suddenly in anger, for what should have been done and hasn't been done. And there are more and more young, and they are more and more restless.

There are leftists.

Take the student business. The students are the sons of the privileged, nobody cared much when they started. As nobody cared when the students came to the factories, distributing leaflets which were not so stupid. The union didn't want them and maybe goes too far, maybe that is wrong but the union wants unity . . .

But the young got the message, and some others too, one can't say they are wrong.

The students wanted the universities, fought for them, and have taken them over. They say the Sorbonne is open to the workers. The students say that they are as oppressed as the workers, and in order to end the oppression once and for all, they need the workers to join them and take over the factories. 'The strong hands of the workers must now take the torch from the fragile hands of the students' (Maoist banner).

T W E L V E

We won't ask
We won't demand
We will take
and occupy
(SORBONNE AMPHITHEATRE)

Aircraft-construction plant. Near Nantes. A few dozen young workers left their machines and called others to join them. The others followed.

Two thousand workers are now occupying the factory. Head manager and aides have been locked up in their offices. Dozens of students have come from Nantes and are staying with them for the night.

As simple as that.

The news reaches the Sorbonne. Sessions are interrupted to give the announcement. The Sorbonne is delirious.

Some archangels are said to have cried.

Cleon. Seine Maritime. Renault factory: gear-boxes.

Two hundred workers (young) refuse to leave the factory after their shift, lock the head manager in his office and stay for the night.

As simple as that.

Flins. Not far from Paris. Renault factory. They have heard the news. The factory is occupied.

It's now Thursday morning, after the Monday of the demonstration.

George Séguy (C.G.T.) telephones Eugène Descamp (C.F.D.T.).

The snowball becomes an avalanche.

Who has taught them rebellion?
Not the unions, but their condition.
Who has told them to take action?
Not the unions, but the example.

Thursday afternoon. Boulogne Billancourt, outskirts of Paris. Renault mother factory (the worker's Sorbonne?).

Atelier 70. A young worker leaves his machine, saying: 'I have had enough.' As simple as that. 'I have had enough.' 'You are mad' – says his mate. 'Oh come on, come along' – he says. He calls the others. In half an hour workshop 70 is idle.

The news spreads throughout the factory. And again, another stops, workshop 72, and again another – workshop 73.

The older workers, the union members, say they should wait for the union 'orders'.

But they are bypassed, in an hour a thousand have stopped, the *responsables* have to stop with them.

And the unions too, they have to play along. They are now scared, very scared, and take the only possible course of action, they jump on the bandwagon. Billancourt is occupied too. But it's the union members, the C.G.T. members mostly, who take over, form the strike pickets, organize the occupation, and fix upon the demands, which come from the union headquarters.

Early afternoon. Friday at Sorbonne: general assembly. The students decide to send a deputation to Billancourt.

At five, C.G.T. leaflets circulate, in and around the Sorbonne. They say: 'We greatly appreciate . . . are opposed to any ill-judged initiative . . . refuse any external intervention . . .'

The C.G.T. The working-class police. The last bastion. The barrier. The last defenders of the bourgeois order, now threatened by all. Two thousand leave the Sorbonne, pick up people at the Odéon, and down towards the South West.

They are the archangels: the spider's thread must become an umbilical cord, between the Sorbonne and Billancourt. Long, long miles towards the periphery of the town, towards Paris' red belt, the sleepy midwife of history, suddenly awake after a hazy dream of years.

The 'popular' districts. Bistros. Bowling. Moralities tempered by life of toil. Ties of solidarity, communities. Each one to his work, immutable universe. Now it's dark. Ghettoes. The fertile dung of the industrial soil, the wretched of the earth, the last to join the banquet, the immigrants from the backwaters of other centuries, from fascist Spain, from fascist Portugal, from desperate North Africa, from the Balkans.

The factory is an island on the Seine.

The last hundred yards.

A lorry, across the road, barring the way. Loudspeaker. On the lorry: a C.G.T. official.

The last screen, the last mystifying ring.

'Thank you for coming . . . appreciate solidarity . . . please no provocation . . . don't go near the gates as the management would use it as an excuse to call the police . . .'

Slowly and deliberately, they pass, on each side of the lorry.

Factory. Metal gates. Bolted. By the C.G.T.

Bars at the windows. The workers, inside, behind the bars. Occupiers, prisoners. Red flags.

Students wave. Workers wave back. Students begin to sing the *Internationale*. Workers join in.

Rhythmic chanting: 'the factories to the workers.'

In the darkish square, which reverberates the chant.

From the factory roof, a lone voice: 'the Sorbonne to the students.'

The walls of Jericho.

Other voices join in, on the same roof; others pick it up, on other roofs.

Silence.

Voice of a student, chanting: 'the Sorbonne to the workers.'

A bucket on a rope is lowered: bottles of beer, cigarettes and leaflets are put in it. They will talk to each other through barred windows. Too young to be lovers.

The Montagues and Capulets are strong, all powerful, mortal enemies and yet – friends in complicity. At other gates, contact is more
difficult. The pickets outside are made almost exclusively of party
members, C.G.T. members, the ones who do not talk.

THIRTEEN

There are no revolutionary thoughts,
only revolutionary actions
(NANTERRE)

Renault, Nord and Sud Aviation, Berliet, Rhodiaceta. The geology of rebellion follows a predictable pattern. A stream rushing down the mountain, cascading, finding its bed and becoming a torrent, then a river.

A patiently woven tapestry. Its outlines only too well known in provincial police headquarters and union offices. Maps drawn with the same care and attention. Since 1936.

Line by line. Retouching here, adding some black there . . .

Maps lying in the bottom drawer of the office desk of the man with the Legion of Honour, of the man with the seat on the Central Committee.

Under lock and key.

Strikes are admitted, strikes are permissible, passing illnesses, a few degrees of temperature, local disturbances, adjustments.

Occupation of factories is dangerous, a challenge, a threat. Workers can threaten to smash the machinery, and the threat alone can prevent any armed intervention.

Masters of the factories, their condition of dispossession is their very strength. The machines, the Capital, owned by others and by others manipulated, are now in their hands. The threat to sabotage them paralyses their enemy, but smashing them would be a suicidal act.

On the other hand they can keep everything in perfect order, preparing for the second stage, the final act, when with the support of workers of higher echelons, they themselves can start the machines running again: workers' power. The Central Committee of the C.G.T. spells out very clearly that they are not calling a general strike, C.F.D.T. will have to follow.

They will ride the tiger, straitjacket the workers into a purely quantitive struggle, appealing to their penury and using it as a bribe and an arm. Asking for a 10% rise, which is needed, of course, very much needed, and getting ready to bargain, very quickly, as quickly as possible, section by section.

The occupation of the factories, started without them, against them, is for them mortal danger. They will have to ride the tiger.

Now the country is in a state of suspended animation, waiting for the inevitable spreading of the strikes (and occupations of factories).

The Sorbonne, and all other universities, have become factories of ideas, the spider's thread is now a spider's web, silver webs into factories.

Paris is joy and bewilderment.

Students' and teachers' unions decide to go and demonstrate in front of the television and radio building; plastic vault which keeps the sky out.

The C.G.T. and P.C. react savagely and threaten.

It is obvious that the militants can go and take over the building (the media, the only and last tool of the present waning power) unless the *flics* are ordered to shoot. (Would they? Could they? Could the government do it? And if they would. . . .)

Students' and teachers' unions have to back down.

Prime Minister calls de Gaulle and implores him to return from Rumania.

A company of C.R.S. has refused to be taken to Paris. The C.R.S. Union is very uneasy: ten thousand reservists of the gendarmerie are put on the alert.

And the tapestry shows its naked pattern. Alice-France goes through the mirror, a mirror which for years had been there in the bourgeois dining-room. But nice people don't think of going through mirrors.

The fall is long, long and easy, one has the time to think. Renault, Berliet, Rhodiaceta, Nord and Sud Aviation have begun.

Now the airports, the shipyards. Railworkers, miners. We are almost there.

Big craters, small cracks, fumes and sparks, boiling waters. The eruption. The crust isn't solid any more. Paris public transport is still. There, the heart, the pump has ceased to beat.

The country is grinding to a halt. Electricity, gas. We've arrived.

Radio and television. The technicians and journalists are restless. It's their consciences.

The French troops stationed in Germany are alerted.

De Gaulle comes back.

Over two million strikers, early Sunday.

De Gaulle finds the words: 'la réforme oui, la chienlit, non' (reforms yes, shitty mess, no).

At Billancourt, they stage a show.

The only masters left (C.G.T.) offer bread and circus to the masses.

Sorbonne and Censier have become the ministry of information of the people.

They produce leaflets, to be distributed to the factories and the provinces.

Naked, limpid, essential. 300 words, no more.

The workers come, discuss their grievances with the students.

A text is discussed, printed, sent. The workers come to tell the reaction of their mates, the text is rewritten.

The university is the factory, the factory a university.

At Beaux Arts: the posters. The workers propose the subjects, the students, the students draw (no artists, no artists, they are all students of the revolution, graphic section). A vote chooses the best to be printed. The cultural revolution is won.

Action Committees. In a geographical area, district of a town. Liaison committees, student-workers. Action committees in factories, professions, offices. Embryos of 'people's power' and vehicles of the expression of direct democracy.

The archangels know by now that the ancient and fallen power has only the police, for very limited actions, the army, for demonstrative action, and the mass media. The first two are totally inadequate, and both are insecure. The third can be beaten, during the action, by leaflets, posters and the direct participation of the people, through their Action Committees.

The real power, the C.G.T. and the reluctant C.F.D.T., can be beaten, in time, if the magic ring thrown around them can be broken.

A movement is beginning to crystallize around militant students, militant workers, some teachers and a fraction of the population. Its immediate aim, extension, consolidation and politicization of the strikes and occupations of the factories. Its main enemies, the C.G.T. and Communist Party.

Its potential allies: the factory workers, first.

But Marx was risibly right. In a state of advanced industrialization, the capital, or rather, the control of the capital, and therefore the power of decision, is in the hands of very few.

Who decides to produce what, how, when and for whom and to what purpose?

Not only the workers of the factories, but all who work for their living, at professional level, however high, haven't any decisional power. In that sense, they are all workers in a gigantic factory called capitalist society, or bourgeois state. They are all exploited, the workers are poor, but the others are too, because they are instruments of alien orders. Direct action (strikes) and direct democracy (strike committees which become committees to change the aims and nature of their work) will have them (from the scientists to the civil servants) as enthusiastic participants. The second ally. There, it's not the C.G.T. to close the ring, and the minds, but the old conditioning. Their discovery is new, their pretence of being privileged, well-off as opposed to being poor, very old.

F O U R T E E N

When the last capitalist will be hanged
with the guts of the last reformist,
humanity will be happy
(LYCÉE CONDORCET)

Citroën: concentration camp factory.

Black uniformed guards at the door. Inspection on entry (subversive literature). Threats, victimization for union activists.

On the production line a Portuguese, a Frenchman, a North African, a Yugoslav and a Portuguese again. So that they cannot talk to each other. Behind them, guards.

Identification cards on them, for spot checks. At the end of the line, a Citroën DS. A car for ministers. Its shape, and style, and character is the expression of the world which produces it. A car to be hated. Its menacing self-assurance (it glides silently) is designed to produce awe.

Monday morning. 5.45.

The factory police are already in: guards, inspectors, little bosses.

At six, the workers arrive. If they go in, no strike. Inside, they are inmates. A strike picket is needed. The workers cannot risk it.

It means the sack later.

The students are there. They, with the most militant, make the barrier. Crowd.

Loudspeaker: 'We are asking you to strike today for the thousand francs, for a work contract (no victimization), pension at sixty. . . .'

Forty per cent are Arabs, Spanish, a past of desperation, a present of more tolerable hell.

What do the students study? Yes, they study Spanish as well . . .

'*Trabajadores todos unidos* . . .'

Company trucks still discharge their human cattle.

They listen, listen to their language.

Chiefs in grey uniforms look for their pet workers, motion them silently to a side-entrance.

They stay, almost all stay and read the leaflets which are distributed.

7 o'clock.

Now that they are strong, they will enter the factory. Guards take refuge in glass cages. But still shyness, uncertainty.

Centuries of dust to be shaken off, penury, helplessness, destiny, the poor will always stay poor, the powerful powerful, for many, still a ghetto behind them and fear of being sent back to their countries.

8 o'clock. Almost.

Young workers come marching, from a nearby branch of the factory, already occupied. Chanting: '*Berçot assassin*' (the owner). They march in. The others follow. Red flag at the main entrance. The workshops are occupied, one by one. The workshop of the young, Gutenberg, is still locked. A young worker to a student: 'When we call it a prison, you see what we mean, look at the door . . .' (It's a metal door, probably stronger than a prison door, it keeps the machines, which are more important – more valuable – than men, under lock and key). Older union member comes.

'Leave it' – he says – 'it means trouble. . . . Got the rest already . . . can't go too far, let's go talk to the others, yes?'

No answer. And he goes away.

Five minutes later, the young workers force a window, get in, activate the electric door from the inside. The door opens.

Shouts, clapping. Red flag.

Can't go too far.

9 o'clock.

Having taken over, the workers organize maintenance, impeccably.

It's Monday. Over seven million workers are on strike. The country is paralysed.

And if one day, if only one day we would stop working, stop working together, then it will appear to everybody, as clear as the law of gravity, that we alone turn the wheels, and without us, the wheels would stop.

Planes don't fly, ships don't sail, trains don't run, the industries are still. But alive, and ready. Ready to begin again for a new order.

Electricity and gas, the blood of the country, are still distributed to the homes of the people.

Water still reaches the taps, electric light the lamps, and gas the stoves, because the life of the people must go on. Only, history must change.

But the grip of the unions is still iron.

The teachers and the students are learning from each other, and helping the workers to teach themselves.

But the unions' ring is hard to melt, difficult to break.

Banks are closing their doors. Politicians are closing their eyes.

People have less and less money, and more and more friends. Frantic insects jump into their cars, pursuing actions with no scope, following the call of lonely cares and fears.

Paris is jammed, one big, lovely traffic jam which finally glutinates into one metal body.

The undertakers are on strike, the dead wait for the new era, too.

Shopgirls suddenly discover that their pay is very poor, their feet very tired. They take over the chain-stores.

The actors join the act.

At the National Library, too many people, too few seats.

Somebody rises from his books and proposes a petition.

The astronomers at Meudon are on strike, not for money, for more stars.

Money is getting scarce. The Bank of France doesn't print notes any more. Bank clerks feel the sting too. They strike. Few counters are open, at the banks, and long queues. But Paris, and the towns still get their daily food. Convoys of lorries bring it from the willing countryside to the hungry towns.

Rubbish isn't collected, mail doesn't arrive.

Differences surface, and likenesses. Stripped of their veils, ancient patterns are now raw flesh.

(A friend, lycée student, rings his home every evening telling his parents not to worry, he isn't hurt and the revolution is going fine . . .)

The strike and occupations of factories and places of work.

They are for bread, dignity, democracy.

C.G.T. claims they are only for bread.

C.F.D.T. says they are for bread and dignity (a change of social structure is very timidly envisaged).

The archangels, and the constellation of stars gathered around them, the movement, claims it's for democracy, yes, direct democracy by the working people.

Workers' committees, workers' councils.

Action committees, local councils.

They are working in depth, within the communities, within the factories.

The C.G.T. is now terrified.

It lies, it cheats, it insults, it threatens.

It uses demagogy: stick to the money. Bread, bread, only bread.

Racism and nationalism: the students, the leftists, they are dangerous, paid by the government, paid by foreign powers, aliens.

It foments class hate: the students are the sons of the rich. But the ring weakens every day.

Working-class districts plunge into the nineteenth century. Bistros, local shops which sell on credit. History is taking its holiday.

The middle classes are hazy, vaporous. Some participate at their place of work, some in the action committees. Others shut themselves up: ostriches.

Their sons are building new firmaments with fragile instruments.

Some are only building a new university, the impossible castle which no police will ever enter, where no authority will ever impose its will.

The best are living the future, and preparing for it in a fever.

The realization that the country is not rotting, only because the workers keep the essential services going, sinks in too slowly.

The unions take the credit, and the Party, ready to hand back everything to a now non-existent State, and to ask for a share.

The papers do their job: lie.

They keep the bourgeois fears alive in those who still have them, and talk about parliament, the ghost.

The peasantry has many grudges, a fraction joins the movement.

For most, the roots are strong, but the sky not too far.

Some will join the workers. At Nantes, the first people's town will be possible. Elsewhere, they'll throw potatoes on almost empty highways.

Petrol gets scarce and disappears.

The long hand of the masters.

No petrol: communication will be difficult for the movement that is now gaining terrain and footholds.

And the bourgeois, the last scared specimens of a once powerful race will not be able to run away with the luggage-boot full of banknotes.

They take refuge in countryhouses, behind closed shutters, guarding the family silver.

Poor old Marx, who liked bad literature and discovered a few elementary truths still finding their way, really said it, in resonant words: The bourgeoisie will disappear. The bourgeoisie of Zola, the shopkeepers torn apart by the maddened populace, the arrogant and ignorant owners of souls and factories, the ministers of morals who administer the goods of the better-off have almost evaporated.

They have left computers, balance sheets, company graphs, exoterically ruling the mystified classes with clinical imperfection.

The bourgeoisie Balzac created between innumerable cups of coffee, through a hundred exalted nights, is now a shadow of itself.

Young cohorts of technicians and scientists raise their slide rules in fascinating mimicry of the century-old gesture of the clenched fist. With their tidy white coats and blurred minds, they are asking for the right to 'decide', to run their own test-tubes and their lives. The small, the small in mind, the ones who own little and that little in fear and stolid pride, they are hoarding food: ants of a revolting species.

And the dregs, at the bottom of the barrel.

The poverty-stricken with no hopes nor understanding, chained to a handkerchief of land, to an archaic job, to the immutable mystiques of King and Country, the opium of the wretched of the earth, and the absolute mystique of possession and its hellish images, the bit of land, the four walls, a secure job, respectable furniture, a black suit on Sunday, daughters virgins, sons respectful (soldiers, policemen, paras). The areas of darkness, where kids grow up to become black *flics*.

FIFTEEN

Run forward Comrade, the old world is
behind you
(ON A WALL OF THE COMMUNE)

Ten days of happiness already
(SORBONNE)

And hour by hour, shift by shift (the workers in the occupied factories have learned that the 'shift-vigils' can't be longer than four hours) day by day, the measure is filled.

At Nantes, students, workers and peasants have joined hands. The peasants enter the town on tractors, with red flags. Action committees and strike committees both become councils of the people.

Factories producing cattle food are reopened, and dairies.

The councils control food prices. Housewives with red bands on their arms check the shops. Councils start organizing distribution of food themselves, at minimal prices. A new power is born.

At Nantes, at Caen, at Saint-Etienne, the prefects of police, barricaded in their headquarters with a few hundred mercenaries, are waiting for the last telephone call. Some printing presses, taken over by the workers, are printing the Sorbonne leaflets.

In factories where half are blue-collar workers and half white-collar workers, both on strike, they are talking of how to run the enterprise together, and to what purpose. A factory producing electronic material is now making walkie-talkies for the comrades.

But factories are only pieces of a puzzle. Most produce only parts, pieces of a product. Many in which the workers have discovered workers' powers, are for the moment useless, not necessary to this dawn of the new communities.

The division of labour, the oldest curse of the working man, is now his mortal enemy. Production and machinery are organized and geographically distributed in a fashion alien to his new and living interests.

The C.F.D.T. plays its timid role.

The C.G.T. plays the police role.

It still has a strong grip on the workers in the essential services. The bastions which it has built through the quiet years: railway workers, miners, post-office workers and above all, electricity and gas workers. It holds on grimly, desperately, while the world, its world, is crumbling all around.

It prevents the running of the trains which must now take potatoes (potatoes, eternal food of the poor) from Finistère where they accumulate to the workers' canteens where they are needed.

And yet, as the days go by slowly, visibly and invisibly, the pendulum swings towards direct action.

The paleolithic communist monster is now immobilized, only its nostrils exhale venomous fumes.

Small, terribly active people are buzzing at incredible speed around its once majestic body.

The vulture screeches, flapping wet wings in a sky filled by lightning.

61 thousand *gendarmerie nationale* (16 thousand with tanks and armoured cars).

10 thousand reservists.

83 thousand police (13,500 are the black C.R.S.).

168 thousand soldiers. 120 thousand are conscripts. Totally unreliable, already confined to barracks for fear of 'contagion'. A contagion which has started already. There are action committees among them.

The non-commissioned officers are students, the soldiers are young peasants and workers. Of the 48 thousand professional soldiers roughly half, under the command of General Massu, are sure.

But Massu isn't, yet.

The paras, the mythical parallel force, is now a few thousand desperados roving the countryside: the twilight of dead gods. The atrophied brain of the C.P. dinosaur sees the danger of extinction. The C.G.T. barrier is cracking.

Lava streaming down the mountainside picks up speed: the glacial era is about to end.

The brain emits frantic signals, the vulture receives them. C.F.D.T., new gazelle still frightened by old monsters, too fragile to hope to survive alone, had to align itself.

Both will talk to the vulture.

The *son et lumière* stage is spotlighted for an instant.

The 'censure motion' of the so-called left is defeated.

Politicians play their violins. The orchestra beats on impassively, while the ship sinks.

But the *son et lumière* must go on at all cost.

On the third floor of the Tour Eiffel radio and television equipment, protected by faithful soldiers, is ready to take the show over.

Parliament recedes into greyness.

Cohn-Bendit is banned from France: the last programme to sustain the *son et lumière*.

Because the students will come out in the streets again, naively, beautifully, furiously and alone.

The C.G.T. and C.P. will watch from a distance: the enemies of my friends are my enemies.

And again it's fighting. Boul Mich is a battleground. Rue des Écoles has good barricades, three comrade trees help.

The black uniforms attack from the bottom of the Boul Mich, as usual. A strategy emerges. Barricades shouldn't be too near to each other, and cannot be kept for long. Between them, fifty yards or more.

The enemy front line, shielded and masked horrors, are heavy and clumsy, as if coming from other worlds. By the time they scream and attack, the defenders should have already left, and be entrenched in the barricade behind, and bombarding with all they have.

Diversionary tactics are essential, if the enemy has to be slowed down. It can be slowed down, temporarily arrested, but not beaten in a war of position, because of their superior firepower and organization.

The defenders chant: 'We are all German Jews', since Cohn-Bendit is, as the Communist rag has pointed out at the very beginning of it all.

Fighting goes on till the last barricades, and later. But is it still worth it? To accept the confrontation in the small arena of the Latin Quarter, the only terrain in which teargas and plastic savagery can impose its force? In the police stations, beatings, humiliations, cries. Is it still worth it to provide them with a false image of victory, when everywhere else the black insects could not move, or show themselves?

It is, because every defeat is a victory, every cry in the Beaujon 'concentration camp' where prisoners are taken to be beaten is a cry for help, which reverberates through consciences. But it isn't, because it provides the vulture and the dinosaur with a fictitious tournament, mystifying the people into believing that the clamour of those clashes is the only sign, the only reality.

Wednesday is fighting, and Thursday is fighting, and now the students try to avoid it, because now it's the time to prepare quickly and patiently the new order of the life to come. But fighting goes on remorselessly. Like the fish in the pond of the Chinese fable, the young might lose battles, but they reappear everywhere.

At the Sorbonne, now also a hospital, a hand has written: 'Ten days of happiness, already.'

SIXTEEN

Freedom is the consciousness of our desires
(PLACE DE LA SORBONNE)

Friday, May 24th.

The press office (is there still one?) of the Prime Minister (there is still one) announces that the unions, Capital and the government will negotiate away the workers' faith.

The ghostly will of government will be mediator.

Quickly, the blade of the knife enters, quickly and swiftly.

Trembling hands are sweating, it might be too late.

The C.G.T. asks all the faithful today to the last celebration, before the slaughter.

High mass is celebrated, in 'order, calm and dignity'.

The vulture retracts its claws.

Flics watch from a respectful distance. They are not needed.

Nantes is already a free town. The main square, ex-Place Royale, is now called 'Place du Peuple'.

In Paris the C.G.T. gives thanks for the attendance, and dismisses the faithful.

A good procession.

But times are hard and dangerous.

The C.F.D.T. has joined hands with young students and workers, who demonstrate their anger. Some of the faithful from the previous mass will join the participants, deserting their church.

Assembly point: Gare de Lyon.

There de Gaulle will be heard on a thousand transistors, saying, amid sarcasm, that he calls for a referendum as to what he should do about all this trouble.

People wave handkerchiefs and tell him to retire.

It's eight o'clock, de Gaulle is one century and a hundred barricades behind. The voice from the grave, asking for the last embrace.

Flics are there, barring the way, blocking the exits.

The demonstrators are bottled, the leaders understand.

The vulture in agony has made a blood-pact with the dinosaur.

With all the strength the power-vulture has left, it wants to fight where it can.

Again a show spotlighted by the media, to make people forget that everywhere else it is powerless. Grass to the sheep.

The battle is inevitable. This time they are fifty thousand.

They are stronger, bolder. They acknowledge the trap, but have to accept the fight.

Their past is their future. The cries are ancient: '*À la Bastille*'.

The same Bastille that two hours ago saw the peaceful C.G.T., the same Bastille.

Hasty barricades. The *flics* charge. People disperse rapidly, covering their retreat.

The second ancient cry: '*À l'Hôtel de Ville*', the cry of the Commune.

Battles will be engaged all over town. In Haussmann's boulevards, which the bourgeoisie made a century ago cutting the popular districts into pieces.

At Les Halles, where unmolested lorries carrying fruit and vegetables still reach their destinations and then slowly, back to the magic quarter. Réaumur Sebastopol is scattered fighting. Faubourg Saint Antoine is fighting sporadically.

The *flics* are protecting the Hôtel de Ville, with the very best they have got. Around Place de la République, thousands of workers are

leading the battle. Leather jackets, the young unemployed, are desperate and efficient.

People come out of their apartments.

The *flics* are guarding the Élysée, the ministries and the buildings
stuffed with documents.

The stock-exchange is undefended. At 10.30 it's invaded.

Purifying flames linger on there, the beginnings of the fire illuminate
silhouettes and a black flag.

Guerrilla warfare is paying off. The enemy's superior 'fire power' is
incapable of coping. At Les Halles, the police station is sacked.

But the advantage isn't exploited. Too many are fighting their way
back to the Latin Quarter, the magic quarter, the citadel. Habit has won
over the imagination. The Latin Quarter is an arena and a trap.

There the *flics* attack from the bottom of Saint Michel, as before, as
usual. Slowly but inexorably they work their way up the boulevard,
through the gas and flames. The war of position can never be won.
The fighters have nothing left but determination and courage, and
barricades as high as their hopes, smashed by bulldozers, enormous
locusts.

They are left their youth, their streets, their despair. Barricades fall
and others are made. Terrain is lost, but fighting goes on. There is
anguish in the night while the *flics* slowly gain footholds and control
and the arrogance.

The Sorbonne is a hospital, the thousand resisters risk massacre.

And yet they continue to assemble, in hundreds, in dozens.

The night punctuated by explosions, by fires.

The minister of hate howls from a radio: 'Paris must vomit this mob
in revolt.' Commandos are still waging battle.

The night is naked flesh.

The last resisters see dawn at Denfert, where demonstrations begin.

They will take refuge in the Montparnasse cemetery, hiding among
the graves.

The Paris Commune has not fought alone.

The *flics* have attacked in Paris and Lyon, where they were strong.

Over most parts of the country, in towns and villages, they have kept out of the streets, barricaded themselves in police stations.

At Nantes, after a long attack on their headquarters, a C.G.T. leader has renounced his church. Negotiations began talks, and the *flics* started talking to the enemy.

Latin Quarter: morning.

SEVENTEEN

to bargain is to capitulate

Latin Quarter: morning.

Young people dismantle barricades in Saint Germain. Some cry.

Clouds of tear gas hang heavily over the battlefield.

Young conscripts are clearing the way in Saint Michel. Watched closely by *flics*.

We smile at them, they smile back.

In the light of the miserable morning, amidst the ruins, after the hours of terror which always follow the *flics'* victories, the Commune knows that its two enemies will try quickly to close the ring around them.

At three o'clock grey Citroëns bring dark-suited men to rue Grenelle, ministers, mediators, masters and union men. Indistinguishable, livid with worry, men in a hurry. union men are skilled chemists of crumbs. Responsible men full of responsibility, who understand the imperatives of the economy, the demands of the market, foreign competition.

First: the minimum salary, to remove their pretext of discontent.

They understand each other. Occasionally, voices are raised. Old habits die hard. And appearances must be preserved, among civilized men.

3 hours 45 minutes and the minimum salary goes up from 384 francs to 520 francs.

The masters are generous, with the workers' money, when it's a matter of self-preservation.

They are now 'working' round the clock, with a very reconstructive spirit.

Sunday comes, and the day of the Lord finds the negotiators still hard at work. 7% now, 3% in October. Or 6% now, and 4% in November?

Forty hours a week? That's just for the slogans outside the factory. Pensions at 60? As a slogan, it has been a useful one. It showed that the unions look ahead. Social security has been curtailed by the régime, in its happy times.

Can we give something on that? Not really. It's all in a day's work.

Bargaining is a sweaty business, but a business all the same.

As long as they both stay in business. Hours drip away.

An unobtrusive old man, the boss of the bosses, makes rapid calculations on a piece of paper. Bribes are never expensive.

Sunday is suddenly gone. Agreement is reached.

EIGHTEEN

no

Billancourt. Monday morning. 7.45.

Fifteen thousand workers are waiting. Defiant mood.

The C.G.T., newly-appointed sergeants of the masters, will bring the news of the 'negotiations'.

To hold their troops, the C.G.T. have used the decades-old armoury, the claims advanced in 1936, still to be met.

Forty hours a week, pension at sixty, freedom of action for the unions and an 'adequate salary', a thousand francs at Billancourt, now.

George Séguy, general secretary of the C.G.T., is coming.

And Benoît Frachon, the president who is 73, and who signed the 'Matignon Agreement' in 1936.

The two generals are afraid. They are bringing nothing but some money, and know that the troops are restless.

Séguy walks through the still crowd, to the platform.

A flamboyant start: 'This is what we have snatched from them, after extreme difficulty, difficult talks. . . .'

The workers listen impatiently to Séguy talking about the magnitude of what 'they' have snatched from 'them'. The waves carry his voice to other factories . . . Billancourt is the house of mother Renault, the biggest, the first to decide, the one where the C.G.T. is strongest, the test-case. Against those who want to break the bars of the cage, Séguy is bringing the stuff to gild them.

He is eloquent, used to translating the imperatives of the masters into the necessities of the masses. Social realism. Decades of speeches after marches, before dispersal.

Séguy makes a slip.

'It has been particularly difficult to get from them strike pay, but after much pressing . . . half will be given and for the other half, there are ways of working for it. . . .' The booing lasts eternal moments.

Séguy, a small man alone in his smallness, begs: '. . . not in your case, in your case you don't need to recover the hours with overtime. . . .' The remark is ignored by the men.

Billancourt says no. They will fight on.

And the other Renault factories say no, and Citroën says no, and Berliet says no and Rhodiaceta says no. No, because not even money is enough, no because the factories are concentration camps, no, because they have discovered their strength, no because, above all, they want something else.

At Billancourt they chant: 'Workers unity' drowning his words.

The chant silences Séguy. The Sergeant Séguy. The high priest of the rites of holy compromise which means submission and acceptance of their present status, of the status quo.

The workers say no. They say no to the unions because of interminable years spent preaching revolution (less and less) and teaching resignation (more and more).

The country has heard the workers' verdict.

It's lunchtime.

Servants spread immaculate cloths over long tables, in stately houses.

Workers cut their bread with knives.

NINETEEN

Workers' Councils
(LEAFLETS)

The general will against the will of the
General
(POSTER)

The workers' No brings controlled delirium to the Sorbonne.

The electricity comrades show their anger in a tangible way. They cut the electricity supply intermittently, in Paris.

It's the absolute arm of the workers, they can plunge the world in darkness. An arm jealously kept hidden by the C.G.T. dinosaur until now.

The Minister of hate, Fouchet, talks of hidden arms depots . . . hints of the shooting which might come . . . threatens. . . . Students, teachers, young workers, all the archangels of workers' control and militants of the order to come need to see each other now that the No has been pronounced, to talk of the immediate present, of the future at hand.

At Charléty Stadium, in the Cité Universitaire, far from the Latin Quarter of the past battles, the enemy's provocation.

The C.G.T., with C.P. support, calls the faithful to meetings at predetermined points. The troops will now be told that time has come for a popular government.

Paris is tense. The masters feel that the C.G.T. has failed them, the last screen has gone. The carcass of society lies bare.

(Maybe if they can shoot very quickly, at the very right moment, so quickly, that the rest will be kept aside by the P.C. shouting 'no violence' and won't have time to come to their support . . . maybe . . .)

But this is only police reasoning. The masters think the government and its police are stupid and dangerous. They have been instrumental in bringing about this revolution, this escalation.

Only one way left, if there is still time, the reasonable one, the C.G.T. one, before the C.G.T. crumbles.

After coffee, presidents and general managers realize, it's almost time to prepare the dossiers for when the communists come.

They have waited for long, now is the time for them to take a share of the burden of keeping the wheels turning.

It'll mean contracts with Russia, it needn't be that bad. Names have changed many times, in this difficult world, they'll change again. And the communists are reasonable men.

Some of the most far-seeing archangels will not go to Charléty but to the communist meeting. Scouts.

Time is very heavy, hanging between past and future, improbably.

Is it possible now to transform all the strike committees into workers' councils?

To start immediately to run the necessary communications and the essential factories – this afternoon?

The light goes out, from time to time, in the houses of the people who stay at home, waiting.

Have the action committees been active enough?

Can they distribute the empty flats, the margins of luxury, to the population of the shantytowns, the margins of misery? Action committees need time, workers' committees need time, time to exist and spread, time to rally potential friends, only a few more days to start a new world.

Most of the fighting has been against ghosts. The *flics* and the stage battles resounded too loudly. The battle of the arena, last week, has provided a plastic setting for the non-participants. The obsessive repetition of the unreal to mask the essential.

The Paris walls said it: power to the imagination.

On the third floor of the Tour Eiffel, guarded by the élite of the army, colonels in charge of three months' supply of films and magnetic tapes are drinking beer.

Night comes to France. Workers sleep in factories, students in Universities, the others just sleep.

The unions will resume negotiations.

At eleven o'clock the next morning, Mitterrand discovers that the government is no more, and proposes a new government. Mendès-France's name is, of course, mentioned. Waldeck Rochet counts the hours. The workers' No must be used to make a special kind of new government, a popular government where the communists will keep law and order, and the workers. The two meet.

Séguy even meets the student leaders, they are needed if a popular government is to be made, frail hands or not. But the ghost of Cohn-Bendit, the symbol of the archangels, prevents any talking.

The ghost is at that moment crossing the Franco-German frontier – frontiers, fuck them! – not in a sealed train-carriage.

And on the stroke of midnight, two hundred McLuhanites are at the Sorbonne press office, waiting to hear the Electric Word.

Cohn-Bendit smiles, the Sorbonne laughs, the nineteenth century recedes imperceptibly, one invisible inch. The skeleton of a new working power is taking shape, spontaneously, but terribly timidly. The dreams of the archangels who envisage it fill the empty spaces and mental spaces.

Nantes' food and mobility are in new hands.

The workers said No to the mess of potage.

The No must coagulate in a concerted action. Time is slipping by.

What the workers call bread, the student-archangels called dreams.

From this dialectic: a new word, and world.

Much time has been spent in mirrors . . .

Comrades, it's Wednesday morning already.

The C.G.T. will bring its men out again, to show the strength of the 'popular government' which is to come, and save the country from anarchy, in the name of the French flag.

De Gaulle has been forgotten, as has his referendum.

Power had the universities. We have taken them.

Power had the factories. We have taken them.

Power has only power. Let's take it.

Heads of cabinet are burning dossiers.

The ghost ministers arrive at the Élysée, for the weekly farce.

An usher tells them the meeting is postponed. It's for tomorrow, at three o'clock.

De Gaulle the general, de Gaulle the plotter, has thrown off the mask.

His Napoleonic disregard for the 'populace', the cannon fodder, cuts through layers of side-issues, cumuli of smoke-screens.

Contempt illuminates.

The eternal shit, the canaille, France's heart has risen from the gutter once again. 1789, 1848, 1871.

Same reasons, same issues, same balance of forces.

The political dialectic between the wretched, the blind sheep who from time to time in French history rebel, and the ageless, immutable mask of power.

You don't seize power, you pick it up.

He has waited, convinced it was a benign cancer. But it's malignant, and it has to be cut out.

People's strength will always be divided, they have hearts but no minds: a pack of fools.

Action must be quick. Justified by a shadow of a threat, the communists will be happy to surrender. Like the nouveaux riches, they want the goods, and the etiquette: the idiots.

France can be saved.

He goes to see the army. The professional butchers are stupid too.

He'll forgive them for his having fooled them once.

Baden-Baden: German territory. The general say yes to the general.

They aren't many, only a handful. But no great general has won through strength alone. Alexander had his phalanx, Hannibal his elephants. Napoleon speed and strategy.

This is not even a battle, just a bluff against a bunch of sergeants afraid of their own troops, and self-castrated. The communists will be more happy than sorry, it will put an end to rebellion in their ranks.

De Gaulle goes to Colombey. Tanks cross the frontier. He parades in the garden. They'll need all night to take position.

The long tentacles of the mass media hang around the walls of his villa.

History, immutable, sleeps.

Only men change. But men are fools.

In Paris two hundred thousand or more sheep have peacefully marched through the streets, asking for a 'popular government'.

Mendès-France, the good man of the hopeless people, has asked for a transitional government.

A few pretorians have been alerted.

The conscripts, the bulk of the army made of worker and peasant soldiers and student officers, are under control.

The night is busy. Pretorians reorganize the paramilitary groups overnight. Trucks converge on Paris.

Strong-arm tactics. They may recoil.

The communists, useful idiots, will step down as easily as they have helped, but the other threat, the unpredictable, seems to be at hand. De Gaulle sleeps soundly now. It's almost dawn.

TWENTY

those who possess in fear and live in death . . .

We will be back
(CENSIER, WRITTEN ON THE NIGHT OF THE POLICE TAKEOVER)

The pretorians have worked well.

Robert Poujade, secretary of the Gaullist party, sounds the trumpet: 'the workers strike for the King of Prussia – he says – the Communist Party. French people should have courage and confidence. The government of the republic will not give in to subversion, the dreams of usurpation will not last long . . .'

Colonels polish their medals. Landladies perfume their armpits.

Paras resurrect their uniforms. Shopkeepers talk to pensioners.

De Gaulle's helicopter leaves Colombey.

A few very visible tanks are taking up positions on the outskirts of Paris.

The radios become grave, and hysterical.

The sportscars of the XVIième find their petrol. De Gaulle will speak at 4.30. The Champs Élysées are getting things ready.

At 4.30 de Gaulle threatens, and launches the holy crusade. The parade of those who fear and own and live in death has started.

Protected by *flics* in black uniforms, channeled by *flics* in raincoats. They parade.

Their fear spawns French flags. Self-preservation becomes self-recognition.

Old men of dirty deeds descend, arm in arm, with men of parchment and voting slips, both escorted by cohorts of valets and servants. Ancestral terrors and recent doubts have poisoned the secluded gardens.

The divine right to property soiled by the nausea of tear gas.

An empty and shiny armour comes clanging down the Champs Élysées, screaming the existence of privilege.

Ghosts, shadows. The progeny of the masters of the machines are only these slaves of the golden calf turned into plastic. De Gaulle nods from the balcony to the distant shouts.

The hours drag.

The mass copulation with fear has left behind its sports-cars hooting obscenities. Young puppets tenderly nursed by midwife *flics*.

Last *son et lumière*. Metallic horns. Bulging car eyes.

The communists, mewing at the door, shivering.

The Sorbonne still stands.

Night and fever. In universities and factories, hopes held against hope.

The C.G.T. will reopen negotiations. The C.P. will talk of working class and votes, of election and votes, of France and votes.

The C.F.D.T. will be bitter and ambiguous.

Mitterrand will spit words.

The Gaullists will organize civic brigades.

Moscow is relieved, for de Gaulle.

Washington wishes success to de Gaulle.

Peking denounces traitors.

At Flins, workers talk of working power, and resistance.

It's the 31st of May, Whit-Sunday week-end.

Power bathes us in petrol.

The first strike pickets are attacked by the *flics*, while the unions sell-out fast.

In the afternoon electricity and gas, the ultimate arm.

For the bourgeois at heart, the great escape to the green fields.

For the populace, Woolworths reopened.

Government, unions and bosses work for them all.

It's time to employ the time-proven craft of strike-breaking.

Archangels shout: 'elections: treason.'

Radios offer lies and soft music.

The light brigades of the mass media point their beams to the sweet emptiness of the mind, to the pleasant pleasures of the body, shells.

A test-case, at Flins. *Flics* attack, workers and archangels mount the last barricades, in awareness and rage.

Repression, misery, impotent, heroism, resistance, agony.

History slows down.

Sorbonne the citadel waves the red flag, hostage of a dream, now defenceless.

Workers back to factories, owned by capital.

Selling labour in order to buy bread.

The rest is invisible, in people's minds.

The price of bread goes up five centimes.

dramatis personae

Working class and bourgeoisie
Old and now overtaken definition for:
(a) those who live meagrely by selling their labour
(b) those who work in privileged positions and conditions and share
the benefit of the 'profit'.

Capital
A self-perpetuating system to produce the means to transform nature.

In order to produce the maximum, it has created the traditional
working class (oppressed) and the bourgeoisie (oppressor), and by so
doing it has prepared its extinction. Working class and bourgeoisie are
now both at the service of capital, and both oppressed by its imperatives. Both want control of their lives. They can take control by direct
action, and abolish the two instruments with which capital rules: the
State and money. Since capital (and profit, its expansion) has hardly
any defenders left, its days are numbered.

The masters
Once the decision makers of Capital. Controllers of its instruments, the
State (politics) and money (economics). Now an almost extinct race,

substituted by graphs and computers, providing the decisions which maximize profit. Estranged executors of the self-perpetuating machine.

The new workers
All those who work, in fields, factories, offices, laboratories and observatories. Living by selling their work (in various degrees of comfort and discomfort) without being able to express their needs, practice their inclinations or fulfil their wishes. Without being able to determine the direction, the aims and the hopes of the community to which they belong.

Communist Party, C.G.T. etc.
The bodies for the amelioration of the condition of the old working class. Once possible vehicles for the overthrow of the old bourgeoisie. Now in alliance with the last representatives of Capital, because they fear extinction in the new order.

The mass media
The means of estranging the new workers from the realization of their submission and the knowledge of their strength. Also the means of keeping the new workers in a perpetual state of haziness, servile hearts, chained to their own possessions. In respect for the old and now empty frame (State and money), in fear of their individual future and without hopes of their collective one.

The young
Without fear of poverty and reverence for property. They have discovered (with different degrees of consciousness) that they must take their future in their hands, by challenging systematically the system. The archangels are the ones aware of the various forms and actions the challenge must take in order to be effective.

The dream
Abolition of Capital, and its profit. And of its expressions: State and money.

Workers control. (The new workers). No delegation of power. Decisions taken by representatives-spokesmen at any time.

All work according to their inclination, necessary toil (machine supervising? manual labour?) is shared by all. No distinction between manual (if any) and mental labour.

All participate in the first, when necessary, and share the second. Self-determination will make the external repressions, State and money, wane and finally disappear.

Then, feelings and concepts yet to be invented.

The archangels

Young (some not) workers and students (some not) who in varying degrees of enthusiasm and understanding envisage the dream and act in order to bring it into reality. The ways are innumerable. Some are urgent.

coda

The tale is exemplary, and also irrepeatable.
Also, France is one single country, but
France is not alone.
The appearances of restoration, historical
hangovers after the ecstasy of the
revolution, do not deter its carriers, do not
deceive its enemies.
When the unpredictable has happened, the
seemingly impossible is at hand.

The signs are many.

JUNE 1968, RUE MOUFFETARD,
PARIS, Vième,
immediately after the events.

why it
happened

TOM NAIRN

ONE

the totally unexpected

As the revolutionary explosion of May 1968 burst upon Paris and the world, a worried editorialist of the London *Times* asked anxiously whether '1968 might even fall into place in French history with 1789, 1848, and 1870?'

In one sense, his anxiety has turned out to be groundless. 1968 did not develop into a revolutionary conquest of power comparable to these other turning-points of French and European history. But in another, more important sense his question was only too well-founded. For 1968 did not fail because it was too weak and secondary an event, a mere accident unworthy of comparison with the great dates. It failed because it was too big, and too novel, and inevitably dwarfed most of the circumstances around it. It was heavy with a significance too great for our times to bear, a premonitory significance which the events of May could only sketch in outline, like a vivid, troubled dream experienced just before waking.

Beyond the dream, in the rest of this century, the meaning of May 1968 will be worked out and revealed in practice, both in France and elsewhere. One of the more obvious lessons of the 'events' was how much more important this is than any theoretical appreciation, or divination of the future. In May, practice led and dominated consciousness, in a surge of collective action. Although the movement threw off a kaleidoscope of ideas, in the debates at Nanterre and the Sorbonne, and on the walls of the Latin Quarter, it was evidently much more than this ideological fury. The ideas express but do not explain it.

> The revolution which is beginning will call in question not only capitalist society but industrial society. The consumer society is bound for a violent death. Social alienation must vanish from history. We are inventing a new and original world. Imagination is seizing power.

So read a poster on the main door of the Sorbonne, on the 13th of May. This extraordinary blend of millenarianism, Marx and modern sociology – difficult enough to decipher in itself – resounds strangely of worlds long past and still to come, in the tenth year of the Gaullist technocracy. Yet this dizzying consciousness was that of a movement which within a few days would lead this real, grimly bourgeois society to paralysis, in the most utterly unexpected revolutionary shock of the twentieth century. The apocalypse prefigured in the dream is already here, under our feet. In this late May of the twentieth century, every brick in our petrified city was shaken in its place, as a secret, haunting dream of release turned into reality for a few moments. And the significance of these few moments lies less in the dream than in the lightning-like revelation that reality itself has altered, towards the dream. How else was such a startling transformation possible? It was not dream but reality that the deepest foundations of the city shook and cracked, as in the first tremors of an earthquake. Describing the last terrible decade in the life of Trotsky, Isaac Deutscher wrote (paraphrasing Marx) that

> This was a time when . . . 'the idea pressed towards reality', but as reality did not tend towards the idea, a gulf was set between them, a gulf narrower yet deeper than ever.*

*The Prophet Outcast: Trotsky 1929–40, p. 510.

Perhaps ours, by contrast, is a time when at last reality has begun to 'tend towards the idea' again.

The author of *The Age of Revolution*, Eric Hobsbawm, has said of the May revolution that

> The events in France are totally unexpected and totally unprece-
> dented. This is the first thing to grasp about them. Practically all
> serious observers of politics have long taken it for granted that
> classical revolutions will no longer happen in the western coun-
> tries. . . . A revolution has never yet broken out under such
> circumstances. Yet in Paris it did.*

This may be the test – and the measure – of a truly original historical development. Every existing theory becomes inadequate before it. Every sacred truth is shown up as partial, in the face of it, and ideas must patiently re-form around it until our awareness has caught up with reality.

Revolutionaries have for long paid a universal lip-service to Lenin's dictum that there can be 'no revolutionary movement without a revo-lutionary theory'. The May upheaval reminded them that there cannot be either of these things without a living revolutionary practice. Without the spontaneity that was the hall-mark of May, revolutionary theory and all attempts at 'planning' or 'direction' are doomed to the archaism and irrelevance now so manifest.

However, it would be equally mistaken to make the facts into a jus-tification for a cult of action for action's sake. For, if spontaneity – the necessarily unplanned breaking of old forms and the old horizons of consciousness – was an obvious lesson of May, it was also the most obvious weakness of the movement. The same shattering unexpect-edness which paralysed the State and the whole of society, and made a total, apocalyptic change seem possible, also held the revolution fatally in check, and made a reversion to established patterns

The Black Dwarf (weekly, London), 1st June, 1968.

inevitable. The rebirth of revolutionary action in western society demands, and needs, a parallel rebirth of theory. No less than previous revolutionary movements, it must depend upon a dialectic of practice and theory. And the whole problem of the 'revision' of revolutionary and Marxist ideas assumes a totally different sense, in the light of what has happened: the familiar deadening conflict between dogmatism and a necessarily 'academic' revision of these ideas is now merely history.

The absolutely necessary struggle towards a more adequate consciousness should not be halted by a recognition that – in Edgar Morin's words – 'We will need years and years to really understand what has happened'.* So we shall, in one sense. But we do not have years and years. In the gathering storm, questions will hardly wait for the definitive answers, in the proper order of library shelves. Willy-nilly, the interpretation of the May revolt has already become a vital problem of the Left, affecting strategy and action. Morin has called it 'une révolution sans visage', the faceless revolution, and the urgency of deciphering the features of this sphinx-visage was evident while the events were occurring, and more evident every day since.

All that the present study proposes to do is to pose certain necessary questions, and suggest some of the terms in which eventual answers may be found. First of all, it is important to ask a simple, fairly straightforward question about the immediate cause of the upheaval: the 'student vanguard'. Secondly, one must inquire more closely into the real character of the revolutionary movement and action itself – especially in relationship to the ideas and practice of the existing, conventional left-wing movements. Thirdly, it is necessary to ask to what extent the revolution was due to specific, French causes and characteristics – to what extent, that is, it may really be seen as a model for other times and places. Fourthly, one must of course at least

*Une Révolution sans Visage, in Le Monde (hebdomadaire), 13th–19th June, 1968.

ask the most important, fundamental question (however limited the chances of answering it are, at this stage): what were the underlying socio-economic causes of 1968, the forces which had secretly moved reality towards the idea?

T W O

the last comedy of capitalism

The revolutionary situation of May was generated by the combative operation of a 'student vanguard' centred on the 'Mouvement du 22 mars'. This vanguard functioned as the 'small motor' of revolution, in Régis Debray's sense.* It is obviously necessary to ask what is the origin of this explosive force. What has made the students, traditionally a quiescent social group deeply integrated into the routine of bourgeois society, turn into that society's most radical element? In fact, as we shall see, it is scarcely possible to answer this question without posing others, that go to the very heart of social reality. However, there may also be a simpler, more superficial answer, which it is worth considering first, as a frame in which to set the later, more difficult ones.

Puzzlement over such questions appears particularly legitimate in France. For until late in 1967 – only six months or so before the revolution – there was little reason to think that anything of the kind should happen there.

---

*v. *Revolution in the Revolution* (Penguin ed. 1967). Debray's theory of revolution in Latin-American conditions (based on the Cuban experience) is that the 'small motor' of the guerrilla force triggers off the 'large motor' of mass popular struggle, by direct actions rather than words and propaganda, or other traditional forms of political organization.

It is true that the French student movement had traditionally a much higher level of political awareness than many others. During the Algerian War (1954–62), it played a significant part in the opposition. This has continued under the Fifth Republic (from 1958 to the present), as is shown by government-favoured attempts to foster a new 'a-political' brand of unionism capable of challenging the consistently embarrassing U.N.E.F. (l'Union Nationale des Étudiants de France). Another constant factor in maintaining such awareness has of course been the many student experiences of violent confrontations with the police, in the course of protests and demonstrations.

However, these forms of consciousness and activity fell mainly within the pattern of conventional Left politics. The more contemporary forms of student action which originated in America and spread to much of Europe in the sixties – 'student power', the techniques of the 'sit-in' and the 'teach-in', the seizure of administration buildings, and so on – were not particularly prominent in France. It is tempting to reproduce in this context the judgment of a leader of the most spectacular single *coup* attempted before May, the Situationist action at Strasbourg:

> In France more than anywhere else, the student is content to be passively politicized. In this sphere too he readily accepts the same alienated, spectacular participation. Seizing upon all the tattered remnants of a Left which was annihilated *more than forty years ago* by 'socialist' reformism and Stalinist counter-revolution, he is once again guilty of amazing ignorance . . .*

*Of Student Poverty: considered in its economic, political, psychological, sexual and – particularly – intellectual aspects, and a modest proposal for its remedy, in a pamphlet entitled Ten Days that shook the University (Situationist International, London). See also Circuit (magazine) No. 6, June 1968, for a better translation of the Situationist manifesto. A Situationist group got itself elected to the students' union of Strasbourg University, and proceeded to dissolve the union and 'put its funds to good use' by founding a Society for the Rehabilitation of Karl Marx and disrupting the official ceremony of the rentrée with a distribution of the above-quoted pamphlet. They were evicted by court order after three weeks of power

This 'ignorance' has been dispelled, more completely and defini-
tively than anywhere else, by the Nanterre agitation and the events of
May. But not, it would seem, as the result of any specially strong pre-
existing tendencies towards that sort of action among French students.
Nor can one look to that other old horse, the French left-revolutionary
tradition, for an explanation. This is, in any case, principally a tradition
of revolutionary *rhetoric*, drastically dissociated from French realities
(on the Left as elsewhere), and it has always been there. No one can
deny the importance of this deeply embedded tradition in the *diffusion*
of revolt, after the motor had been set going. But it cannot help one to
understand how it got going in the first place.

Another prominent absentee on the French scene was the form of
youthful rebellion most developed in America or London: the 'underground', and the Hippy phenomenon of a generalized anti-bourgeois
style of life and language. The role of this element in Parisian existence
was fairly symbolized by the small groups (mostly foreigners) still
taking the sun at their favourite, picturesque *lieu de rencontre* on the tip
of Ile de la Cité in April, and awaiting the first police operations of 'net-
toyage' this season. The police like to keep things (conventionally)
picturesque for the tourists. Thus, there was little precedent either for
the total form of revolution which burgeoned so rapidly in May.

In the absence of these most obvious candidates, the type of explanation which has been advanced most widely is the same as that given
for other student revolts, in other countries: the very bad conditions of
both teaching and student life in French higher education. For example, the last decade has seen a huge increase in student numbers – from
170,000 to over 600,000 – and the provision of new buildings and
other facilities has nothing like kept pace with this increase.
Overcrowding is particularly notorious in Paris (where there are

devoted to (in the judge's words) 'abolition of work, total subversion, and a
world-wide proletarian revolution with "unlicensed pleasure" as its only goal . . .
sinking to outright abuse of their fellow-students, their teachers, God, religion,
the clergy, and the governments and political systems of the whole world.'

around 182,000 students): lecture-halls and libraries jammed to capacity, a grave shortage of student accommodation and inadequate canteen facilities in a city where restaurant eating is impossibly dear. Even *Time* could find a tear or two for the Parisian students, after May:

> Thus, French students often project an image of despair. They constitute a hard-pressed band of impecunious, hungry scholars restlessly roving the Latin Quarter, looking for a warm place in the winter or even a café with enough light to study by.

International reaction has clearly lost the rosy image of the perpetual Parisian *bohème* once so close to its pimply heart. Nowadays, an American in Paris means an army deserter hurling a *pavé* at a policeman.

The impecuniosity of French students has of course the same reasons as elsewhere: the enduring bourgeois prejudice (common to East and West) that education is a 'privilege' of some kind, to be paid for. If not with money, then with misery. Or – more accurately – with a gaily endured insufficiency of means. It was well known, until the month of May, that students (like the early factory workers and the plantation slaves of the Old South) are happy with little, having each other, and their natural *joie de vivre*. Also that one is happier without 'responsibilities', however poor. Then again, why should one not 'pay' for one's future as a trade-marked and guaranteed exploiter with a bit of hardship?

The normal sufferings of carefree youth engendered by this diseased philosophy were also clearly aggravated in France by the exceptionally rigid and authoritarian pattern of higher education. This sector is marked by the same degree of centralization and hierarchy as other aspects of the French State. Ferocious examinations stud the path of the French student and still more that of the would-be teacher in higher education. Professors are God-like creatures, hopelessly deformed by the process in most cases. This highly 'rational' and bureaucratic machine is shaped – more openly and brutally than in most other countries – for the production of an administrative and intellectual élite, and the principal educational development of the Gaullist régime, the 'Fouchet reforms', were simply designed to modernize the apparatus and make it cope with the greatly increased numbers. It was Fouchet, in fact, who spoke of 'industrializing the university' to describe his own work. Gaullist neo-capitalism needed a larger, more varied élite than that turned out by the old system.

But the essential conditions of this formidable brain-factory were not new in 1968, any more than the old French-revolutionary rhetoric, and bring us little nearer to understanding the causes of the revolt. And – more important – one must observe that lists of woes of this sort never explain revolutions anywhere.

Revolutions have rarely if ever been caused by material misery, deprivation or tyranny, even of the extremest kind. Most people, for most of history, have suffered conditions of life and work that seem utterly intolerable to the West of today. Most people in the 'underdeveloped' world still do. They are normally tied into such alienation by an ideological consensus of some sort which makes suffering appear 'natural' and inescapable. Only if this is broken by a sense of some possible alternative does misery become abruptly 'insupportable'. As de Tocqueville pointed out in his classical analysis of the background to 1789:

> The evil, which was suffered patiently as inevitable, seems unendurable as soon as the idea of escaping from it is conceived. All the abuses then removed (as in the Fouchet reform, for instance!) seem to throw into greater relief those which remain, so that their feeling is more painful. . . . The French found their position insupportable, just where it had become better. . . . Imagination, taking hold in advance of this approaching and unheard-of felicity, made men insensible to the blessings they already enjoyed and hurried them forward to novelties of every kind . . .*

*Alexis de Tocqueville, *L'Ancien Régime* (Blackwell ed. 1962), pp. 186–7.

In other words, the problem is that of explaining the origins of the consciousness of misery which, in a very short space of time, made the conditions of Nanterre and the Sorbonne appear in this new light. Why, when, did the Bohemian ethos cease being an effective instrument of adaptation to these conditions? How did the imagination of 1968 acquire the power to detach itself from circumstances sufficiently to again leap forward in this fashion – and create what was in effect the inverse image of all that the French university had been, in the great democratic debates of May?

Authority has always had its debased answer ready for such questions, naturally: that universal resort of the mentally handicapped, the theory of the 'agitators' (preferably foreign) and their unwholesome conspiracy. This banal paranoia of threatened power was fittingly expressed in this case by the French government's treatment of Cohn-Bendit. And later, by their large-scale and brutal expulsion of 'undesirable aliens'.

The ultimate answer to the problem certainly involves the whole of what society has become, and cannot be given, or even suggested, in a few phrases. And yet, there is a proximate, superficial answer which – if it does not take one very far – at least points in the right direction.

It is a simple fact – scarcely of 'history' even, almost of chronology – that the present generation of young people aged 20–25 in Western Europe and North America occupy a unique position in the development of civilization. They are the products of a conjunction of circumstances without any real parallel in the past.

For the first time since the era of the Neolithic villages – and very precisely, in the life-time of the new *enragés* of the Latin Quarter – the historical phenomenon of 'civilization' has attained something like its natural goal. That is, in countries on roughly the same level of evolution as France, it has developed its powers of material production to the point where most people, most of the time, are liberated from the elemental conditions of poverty and scarcity. There is no need to indulge in foolish *images d'Epinal* of happy motorized workers, to underline this point. Both in France and elsewhere, great masses of urban and rural workers remain in fact just above the bread-and-butter line, and have a hard fight to stay there. Nevertheless, nobody can deny that even this is enormously in advance of what the system managed in the past (between 6000 B.C. and A.D. 1950). Furthermore – just as important – it is in this period that a generalized confidence has been created, where for the first time material prosperity is 'taken for granted'. Thus, civilization (in the form of western capitalism) reached what one might describe as its Utopia, a plateau of achievement where – however much remains to be done, here and there – the major barrier had been broken down, and a solid framework made for future advances.

This is not to ignore, or to minimize in any way, the cost of such western attainment. It was done on the backs of the 'under-developed' world, through a machinery of imperialist exploitation still largely intact. It is sustained by a permanent, colossally wasteful war economy that may be essential to its present uneasy equilibrium.

But in the present context, it is more important to observe that these relatively 'external' conditions are not necessarily experienced from within the system (directly, at any rate). Seen internally, the neo-capitalist equilibrium can appear as absolute; therefore, as the foundation of indefinite future progress. Such is the point of celebrated analyses like Marcuse's *One-Dimensional Man*. They present a picture of societies trapped, perhaps irrevocably, in the very conditions which have rescued them from the worst evils of history. Just because they have succeeded to that extent, the primary will to change has vanished along with primary poverty, leaving humanity locked in an ever-more powerful mechanism of secondary alienation. How can de Tocqueville's 'idea of escape' ever explode into these circumstances, how can imagination ever again impel men forward towards 'novelties of every kind'? Thus, it appears reasonable to say (in phrases from a collection of socialist essays published in January 1968):

In the homelands of capitalism where Marx lived in expectation of the overthrow of class society in his own lifetime, it now appears stronger than ever, part of the order of nature.

Or:

> In the foreseeable future there will be no crisis of European capitalism so dramatic as to drive the mass of workers to revolutionary general strikes.*

And if this is generally true, surely it must be most true of young people, who have known nothing but the repressive machinery of 'one-dimensionalism'? It may still be clear to the elderly, who recall the old confusion, or to a few readers of the right literature, that there are other possible dimensions. How can it be clear to the new masses reared wholly within the efficient nightmare of triumphant capitalism?

All the more so, one would have thought, considering that now they are educated, as well as fed. This is one of the most forcible contrasts between the present and the only other era when capitalist society maintained its equilibrium for long, at the end of the nineteenth century. Education was then a matter, on the one hand, of a minimal culture necessary for work and citizenship, and on the other of a refined élite formation affecting only the ruling class and its immediate dependents. Now France, for instance (like other comparable countries) looks forward to a time when about half the population will receive some kind of higher education. Even if the change is still mainly limited to middle-class strata – as in France – it is striking enough. Within the repressive reification of the system, the increase in 'opportunities' is real enough. Surely, this should be the decisive element in tying consciousness into its categories?

The present generation of young workers and students in western

---

* The Socialist Register, 1968: V. G. Kiernan, Notes on Marxism in 1968, p. 177, and André Gorz, Reform and Revolution, p. 111.

society, therefore, should be the most 'integrated' and docile that capitalism has ever known. They have inherited the earth, *en masse*, as no other generation in history has ever done. They live at the end of history, standing in a reasonable comfort on the shoulders of slavery, feudalism, the bourgeois industrial revolution, and imperialism. They have less to complain of than anyone else, and the students – future mandarins of this consumer society – least of all.

So much for yesterday's realism. Perhaps nobody could have known it before. In any case, the matter-of-fact truth is now clear to practically everybody. This ultimate, Utopic generation is *by far* the most revolutionary one the system has ever produced. And it cannot really be a matter of chance that this is so.

Were any other generation involved, one might ask indeed – especially about students – what particular 'hardships' or 'grievances' were behind the trouble. In the actual conjuncture, this is beside the point. Firstly, one would expect the reasonable sons of an 'affluent society' to treat grievances as grievances, not as pretexts for heaping abuse on the régime which made it all possible. And secondly, if one draws up any number of lists of the 'grievances' involved in a typical student action, they never measure up even approximately to what happens. The first thing the movement does is to transcend the complaints from which it starts. It is very obvious that no armful of grumbles comes near to explaining May. But the same thing has been true of every significant student movement, from San Francisco to Warsaw.

The truth is a comedy too deep for laughter, because too shockingly close to the tragedies of history. Here is all that the petrified city can produce, in its most sensitive and privileged heart, the ultra-refined product of the slaughter of billions and the pillage of the globe: a race of violent heretics who are the human *negation* of everything it means. Once, revolutionaries were thrown up by desperation, or by a long, complex process of renegade intellectual formation. Now, they are being mass-produced in the system's brain-factories, by some crazy mis-design of the machinery no one noticed.

But the point is, in this phase of history, the design cannot be accidental, to be put right by the speedy action of a Minister Fouchet or a Warden Sparrow.* If no one noticed, it is because – in a sense – there is nothing to notice. Capitalism has to develop the educational system (and more widely, the forces of mental production) which it needs, to function properly. The contradictory result which is destroying the brain of the system is, itself, the result of a contradiction absolutely built into these forces. The ultimate, 'perfect' bourgeois generation is revolutionary *because* it is 'perfect', the fruit of Adam Smith, Keynes, and many, many Harold Wilsons. Capitalism is generating its negation, and its fate, within its nerve-centres, because it is helpless to do anything else. A simple, anonymous statement by someone from the *Mouvement du 22 mars*, the prime mover of the May revolution, put it best of all: 'Dans un monde d'abondance le jeune européen 68 veut être: un homme total.'† The logic of this is the precise anti-logic of the system which, itself, gave rise to the desire.

In the rue Gay-Lussac, in May, this comedy of our world became tragedy, but a tragedy which crystallized the forces at work into a diagram for the blind to see. The fragmented universe which had laboured so painfully to produce this wish for wholeness, the impossible opposite of itself, turned on its offspring with homicidal fury. The battles were like

> An initiation rite, in the heart of the archaic forest, where terrifying and maleficent spirits must be confronted. Such was the role

*Mr John Sparrow is the Warden (Director) of All Souls College, Oxford. He recently made a plea for stronger repression of student unrest and again betrayed the motives of his own generation by describing rebels as 'sluts, male and female, making love (if that is the word for it) in the streets'. v. article *Revolting Students* (sic) in *The Listener* (London), 4th July, 1968.

†*Ce n'est qu'un début, continuons le combat*, Mouvement du 22 mars (Maspero, June 1968), p. 130: 'In a world of abundance, the young European of '68 wants to be – a whole man'.

of the French State's policemen, who thereby brought about a real initiation to adult life, that is, to the cruelty and bestiality of the world.*

The bestiality of the counter-attack is well described elsewhere in these pages. So is the fact that the younger the initiates were, the harder they fought.

The established order has, characteristically, given little thought to what it will do with those still unborn. Create one C.R.S. for every student? Abolish the university? Allow its educative process to produce 'whole men', who are all the more certain to combat and eventually shatter the shell of alienation? In the same way as, yesterday, bourgeois society remained skilfully blind to the implications of its major horror, the murder of the Jews, today it avoids the consciousness of its own future. In the mountain of words produced around the May 'events', very few focused on the real threat. A wave of student revolutionaries, regardless of what happens in 1968 or 1969, will be everywhere tomorrow – as they were intended to be – with their hands on levers of power. Whether or not the contagion occurs in the direct, electric pattern of May, it is in the nature of student revolt to spread to the rest of the social body, tomorrow.

*Edgar Morin, La Commune Étudiante, in Le Monde (hebdomadaire), mai 16–22, 1968. Reprinted in Mai 1968: la Brèche (Fayard).

THREE

a new subjectivity

In the locus of the May revolution, among the students, a dream of the absolute flowered – apparently impossibly – from the society which had abandoned ideologies for moderate satisfactions of the ego. In the eye of the storm, the social order became its opposite. Yet this is only one of the contradictions of May, the most visible and symbolic, but not the most important.

If one turns to look at the character and unfolding of the revolutionary movement itself, a deeper, more essential contradiction is at once obvious. Beyond the words, and the words that were deeds, lies the quality of action and organization manifest in every aspect of what happened. Underneath the ideas, there is their source: a new subjectivity, a collective 'instinct' of behaviour which, in four weeks of time, emerged from its chrysalis to become the matrix and vision of a new world.*

Again, this subjectivity is the denial of what exists. Capitalist-industrial society (as the apologists of technocracy never fail to

*For an account of an individual transformation, v. *Itinéraire d'un 'enragé'* by Michel D., in *L'Événement*, June 1968: 'J'étais un imbécile, je croyais que la seule forme de révolte qui s'offrait à moi était la révolte individuelle . . .'

remind one) is more 'complex' every day. Its ever more extensive organization – State and private monopolies – demands an ever more intensive specialization of the individual's function. Co-ordinating this increasing mass of fragmented tasks into a single web demands more and more 'management' – in effect, the concentration of the responsibility and initiative taken from individuals into the hands of 'supervisors' or planners (whose 'specialization', in terms of the system's mystification, is directing others). Hierarchical authoritarianism, rationalized and rendered more impersonal, is the 'natural' price the citizen-fragments pay for their blessings. The revolutionary movement, by contrast, aims at the *total* recuperation of what the system drains away. The 'whole man' must feel, and act, wholly. His subjectivity is the instinctive assertion of *control* over what happens: work, 'leisure', life.

What renders this impulse revolutionary is its naturally social character. It is not – and this may be the single most revolutionary element of May – an instinct of individual rebellion, a counter-attack of the ego on the system's abuse. Society is perfectly well adjusted to this kind of reaction. It works as an immense hive of alienation, ever more collective in its organization and working, but ever less social in its human reality. The individual is at once rendered an insect – at work – and a pure, isolated individual outside it. The system depends upon 'privacy' and its dream-industry produces heroic images of individual rebellion to order. They are the ordinary disguising magic of the machine. It knows that the king-size drop-out or square peg is the quintessence of the human: *because* everyone cannot be like Charlton Heston. Hence the most characteristic mis-diagnosis of student revolt by conventional bigotry: for the bourgeois, they are 'selfish', and for the Communists, they are 'adventurers'.

In fact, student revolt is the diametric opposite of both these categories. As far as the bourgeois are concerned, it represents the one thing which the system can never stand: a living sense of collective power, in movement, the sensation of creative group potential. This is the only 'dimension' that matters, the one which every single thing in

the system conspires to exorcise. Hence one of the comic side-shows
of May: the unsparing effort of commentators to find a 'leader', the
one hero-personality which would put everything in perspective. In
the sense sought for, there is none. Cohn-Bendit is the movement's
sacrifice to the outside world's thirst for a face, carried to artificial
prominence by the decision to expel him. In reality, the movement
produces chairmen, not chiefs, and angrily rejects both bureaucracy
and personality-cult.

As far as the Communists are concerned, the failure is infinitely
worse. They fail to grasp its historical significance, as well as its
immediate sociological nature. Student revolt is the self-definition of
students as *workers*. It is the rejection of the entire, ancient, now
phoney category of student-hood, the assertion that intellectual work
is what it is: the fabric of the new society. What misleads the managers of the *Parti Communiste Français* is that this self-definition –
being a free action – is naturally that of the *non-alienated* worker.
This is a creature they know nothing about. He would be less fright-
ening if he was green and had six legs: then one could propose an
official exchange of views, with an eye to peaceful co-existence. But
these are real monsters, walking paragraphs from the *Manuscripts of
1844* and the *Grundrisse*, the living accusation of all that western
Communism has become. They may be a time-bomb behind the eyes
of capitalism, tomorrow. It is the Communists who are threatened,
today.

In this context, they become the soft underside of the system. For
they represent its semi-official dream of sociality, and this dream
instantly becomes a framed and faded image in the light of a real
upsurge of Marx's 'social individual'. They work by being, on the one
hand, the defensive organization of society's fragments which (like
any trade union, like social-democracy) is forced to accept the general condition of fragmentation, and the official distorting mirror
that reflects things whole: parliamentarism. But what distinguishes
the P.C.F. and its union the C.G.T. is that, on the other hand, it has its
own dream to counterpose to alienation. The daily horror is made

tolerable by the sense that this recuperative force runs through it, in the organization, and tends towards the dream. This proletarian dream-machine is superior to Hollywood for two reasons. First, simply because *l'Humanité*, unlike Charlton Heston, projects a dream of collectivity which appears both to reflect and transcend the present, a realistic vision. Second, because there are no criteria for judging real advance towards the vision, from one year to the next. The bureaucratic apparatus judges progress (and sustains confidence) by small, measurable gains, so much money, so many more *députés*, which have no direct relationship to the giant, qualitative change ahead. But it can maintain the feeling that they have the indirect relationship to it of 'tending', or 'preparing'. This illusion of endless tending is fostered, for the Communists, by their role of professional *damnés* inside capitalist society. Because they are forever cast as villains of the piece, they *must* be real ones, in spite of all the evidence to the contrary. . . . But in fact, this is simply their enormous advantage over social-democrats, from the point of view of the system. Society now requires a visible anti-christ more than ever. Britain, with its miserable Communist Party, has to make do with the blacks. France is blessed with a strong Communist movement which can both block revolution and then, immediately afterwards – as in the June electoral charades – function as the whipping-boy of the counter-revolution, the totalitarian menace. In the one-dimensional society, the function of this universal, all-tastes-catered-for prostitute is obvious: to provide the necessary illusion of another dimension. On week-days it keeps the workers content; on electoral Sundays it drags its blotchy carcase to the Élysée, to fulfil a higher function. And always, it deceives itself that this is love, in order to keep going.

The instant that a real other dimension appears, the illusion is shattered. A revolutionary subjectivity wishes to appropriate the world, to master it in the erect freedom that is our nature. It must do it *now*, and it must be *everything*. For the simple reason that where it has been re-born, nothing else is tolerable: in its heat, there are no more abstract truths, or dreams bequeathed to the grandchildren.

Alienation has become an insult, an obscenity. The first product of revolution is truth: not one more foreman's yell, not one more exam is possible.

Because this truth is at the heart of things, everything else finds its own truth in relationship to it, through an implacable re-arrangement of perspectives. There were still some who hoped that the prostitute would have the proverbial heart of gold, in May. In fact, she had lost even the memory of the real thing. This was the true nature of the Communist 'betrayal'.

The old grey mares of Stalinism are currently apologizing for their existence by saying that 'no revolution was possible' in May, that a successful insurrectionary coup was out of the question. As if this was the problem! Whether or not success, a seizure of power, was possible (a problem one could debate), there is absolutely no doubt that the Party of the Revolution could have at least recognized its own, in May, could have generously welcomed the beauty of May, and advanced the real process of revolution in a thousand ways. It could have reached out to the new workers, instead of shutting them off from the old workers. It could have tried to rise to the level of the Italian Communists of fifty years ago, by leading the factory occupation movement and urging the formation of workers' councils. All that could have been asked of these apostles of reasonableness was to exploit the situation in a reasonable, realistic fashion. Instead, they spat phlegm at the revolution until the barricades, and spent the rest of the month building their own barricades against the revolution itself.*

The life of the revolutionary movement contradicts the organized deadness of society. The authentic wealth of human beings reduces material wealth instantly to a drab backcloth of objects. However long the revolution may take, in one sense it always triumphs in a moment,

---

*For the debate on the precise nature of the Great Betrayal, v. Jean Dru, in defence, *Le Nouvel Observateur* 26th June–2nd July, and Serge Mallet for the prosecution, ibid., 15th–21st July.

wherever the heat of its transfiguring sun is felt, wherever the unbe-
lievable riches of the real social body are released. Where wealth
becomes poverty, and poverty wealth, every other contradiction of
society is shown up and driven towards explosion.

The Party of the Revolution is revealed as the Party of Order: its
dream-content of aspirations is contradicted by its conservative form
and organization, and (at least in the case of the P.C.F.) the latter is the
stronger. But the same is true – more surprisingly – of the other,
smaller parties of the revolution, the 'groupuscules' so active in the student and labour movements before May.*

These groups of 'ultra-left' revolutionaries were automatically sin-
gled out by both the police and the Communists as the cause of all the
trouble. In fact, they neither provoked nor led the revolutionary movement. Although they certainly had some influence on its development,
they were on the whole left behind by it. The highly organized, doc-
trinaire 'groupuscules' were eclipsed by the *ad hoc*, loosely-organized
alliance of forces. They are all very consciously the antithesis of the
bureaucratized corruption, the systematized 'betrayal' it represents.
Their positive bond is devotion to the Leninist theory of the highly-dis-
ciplined, avant-garde revolutionary party. The essential purpose of the
party must be to recruit members from within the working class, and
more generally to diffuse revolutionary ideas there. For the working
class is the only possible motor of revolution, an idea which goes back
to the *Communist Manifesto*:

> Of all the classes that stand face to face with the bourgeoisie
> today, the proletariat alone is a really revolutionary class. . . . All
> previous historical movements were movements of minorities, or

*Among the important 'groupuscules' were the Trotskyite *durs*, the O.C.I.
(Organisation Communiste Internationaliste) and their student arm F. E.R.
(Fédération des Étudiants Révolutionnaire); the more 'open' J.C.R. (Jeunesse
Communiste Révolutionnaire), associated with the French IVth International;
and the Maoist P.C.M.L.F. (Parti Communiste Marxiste Leniniste de France).

in the interests of minorities. The proletarian movement is the self-conscious, independent movement of the immense majority, in the interests of the immense majority . . .*

Hence, all political agitation must revolve around the proletariat, or be doomed to futility.

Lenin's modification of this notion consisted in the recognition – after a great deal more working-class organization than Marx himself had known – that proletarian movements by themselves never rise naturally to fulfil their revolutionary potential. Marx's 'emancipation of the working classes' cannot be wholly 'conquered by the working classes themselves'.[†] To pass from the 'trade-union' ideal of obtaining a square deal within existing society, to that of totally changing society, they require the catalytic influence of the avant-garde party. This is usually composed not of workers but of 'intellectuals' from the middle classes, renegades who have undergone the difficult process of revolutionary self-education and become 'revolutionaries by profession'.[‡] Only their guidance and organizing power can transform the 'spontaneous' discontent of the workers into effective revolution. Their consciousness is an essential factor in the formation of the whole class's self-consciousness and self-activity.

But beyond such ideological reference-points, the 'groupuscules' are defined even more sharply by their real, very material character as the products of a certain history. For over thirty years – since the failure of the Great Depression to bring revolution, and the simultaneous rise of Stalinism – groups like these have been the self-conscious upholders of the revolutionary tradition under almost impossible conditions. During the whole of this period, the working class which was the focus of their attention has shown very little tendency to move in the direction they hoped. Reality has not 'tended towards the idea'.

*Selected Works of Marx & Engels, vol. I, pp. 43–4.
[†]General Rules of the Working Men's Association, 1871, Selected Works, I, p. 386.
[‡]Lenin, What is to be done?, Selected Works, II, p. 126.

The evolution of Marxist groups in this era can practically be seen as variations on one theme: where reality does not tend towards the idea, the idea must become reality. And this is perhaps truest of all – because most unconscious – in movements which accept as an article of faith the dominance of material reality over ideas. In the West, they passed insensibly from seeing themselves as the necessary fomentors of revolutionary action, to seeing themselves as constituting the revolution. While the official Communism of the Soviet-line Parties was poisoned by too great an integration into the material realities of bourgeois society, and by subordination to the material interests of the U.S.S.R.'s foreign policy, the dissident groups were poisoned by too great a detachment from these realities. That is, by a visceral idealism every bit as much in contradiction with their ideology as the prostitution of Stalinism.

How could they evolve in any other way? They found themselves hopelessly isolated within a society which had apparently renounced revolution, a fallen world where capitalism recovered from every setback with extraordinary vigour and flexibility. History had persistently taken the wrong turning. The revolution had been channelled into backward countries, and deformed by their conditions. Hence, the 'groupuscules' necessarily became the guardians of the true revolution, the revolution envisaged by Marx, Lenin, and Trotsky, but never realized in fact. In the circumstances, this could only mean guarding the *idea* of the revolution, however vigorously they tried to act. Until May, they remained guardians of the flame, in a world that would not catch fire.

Although the idea was that of revolution, the task of guarding it was a profoundly conservative one. This is the inhuman, lacerating contradiction behind the gross deformations of Trotskyism and other forms of non-Stalinist Marxism. Neither the noble determination with which they defended Marxism, nor the supreme value of their cause, are impugned by pointing out the immense cost of this defence.

Marx defined the 'sectarian' mentality as that which places a higher value on the things which distinguish it from other trends, than on those which it has in common with them. The dissident Marxist groups of the last thirty years have been forced into this grim sectarian mould by three overwhelming pressures. First, by the enormous effort of resisting the general hostile environment of a flourishing capitalism. Secondly, by the unending battle against Stalinism, the official possessors of the legacy of 1917. And thirdly, by the struggle against the most immediate enemy – those other groups who also laid claim to the true inheritance.

Of the three battles, the last has been by far the most utterly destructive of the genuine legacy of Marxism (which has never been, and never will be, the property of one political movement, or of one nation). It was inscribed in the very conditions mentioned that this should be so. For a revolutionary movement, the whole sense of its existence must lie in a permanent contrast between thought and action, a never-ceasing dialectic of idea and practice. Ideas which do not merely interpret the world, but seek to change it profoundly, must continuously and essentially 'revise' themselves in living contact with the world. Where this dialectic ceases – as it did for so long, in the West – the criteria for distinguishing one idea from another are fatally eroded. There can be no revolutionary truth, since there is no revolution. Hence, the world of such ideas became fatally shut in upon itself: arid theoretical disputation replaced the living antagonism of revolutionary debate. Where ideas are all, the upholder of a contrary thesis becomes automatically an enemy – indeed, the most vicious of enemies, since his 'position' is the most direct contestation of the vital truths. Where the revolution is reduced to this poverty, every scrap matters: every opinion, every attitude, every individual adhesion to this or that idea must be fought over like a bone. Antagonism becomes hatred, and polemic is turned into degenerate abuse. While the revolution itself tends to polarize society, so that in time whoever is not with the movement is against it, this vicious caricature of it deliberately turns possible friends into enemies. Thus, it reassures itself daily of the purity of its revolutionary mission. Success is measured by the number of attacks on the sect, especially in the left-wing press, and by their

degree of spite. On a really good day in France, a group of Trotskyite
'*durs*' like the O.C.I. could bask in the spleen of assaults by everyone
from *l'Humanité* to the Situationists, via the ultra-despicable *Le Nouvel
Observateur.*

The more this inverted logic is pursued, the deeper the gulf
becomes between idea and reality. The more absolute, therefore,
must become the confusion of idea and reality in the mind of the
sect. Every idea in time acquires a fetish-like rigidity: and most of
all, the basic belief in the revolutionary nature of the proletariat.
When the workers are not revolutionary, the faith in their being so
is turned into a travesty of itself, the central totem of the anti-
system – in the French term, '*ouvrièrisme*', or 'working-class-ism'.
Ouvrièrisme mechanically denies that any other class or group can be
'really' revolutionary, if it does not subordinate itself instantly and
totally to the working class.* Naturally, in practice this means
instant and total subordination to the sect, since it is alone capable
of leading the workers and (as long as they are reticent) of voicing
their real mind.

With a feverish energy more reminiscent of the Fifth Monarchy Men
and other Puritan sects of the English Revolution than of the
Bolsheviks, the Marxism of the 'groupuscules' clings to the conviction
that history is on its side. It is compelled to have exceptional faith in
the objective 'laws' of the revolutionary process – all well-known in
advance, and repeated every week in the party paper – and in the
inevitable machinery of breakdown that will provide the 'revolutionary

---

*Students are leading sinners in this respect. Thus, on the evening of 10th May,
while the battle was being prepared in the Latin Quarter, the F.E.R. Trotskyites
paraded there and endeavoured to persuade the students to go home, and
leave revolution to the workers. They thus severed themselves from the revolutionary movement in a hail of abuse, at the precise moment – *la Nuit des
Barricades* – which was to be effective in involving workers in the revolution.
Later, the same group counselled its militants to keep well away from the
Sorbonne debates, '*la kermesse de Cohn-Bendit*'. What need had they to go
there, indeed, after demonstrating such total possession of revolutionary truth?

situation'. Gramsci's often-quoted description of such determinism as
'a force of moral resistance against defeat, useful to the masses but
poison to the intellectuals as it leads them into . . . imbecile compla-
cency' sums up this psychology very well.* Since, however, the basic
truth of the situation is just that the iron law of history has ceased to
function for the time being, this faith is not so simple. As Gramsci also
pointed out, it is actually internalized by the strange logic of sectari-
anism, and translated into 'strong willpower and interventionism' –
that is, into just the opposite, a bottomless faith in organization, in the
ability of the group to accomplish by sheer drive and hard energy all
that 'history' is failing to do.†

The fierce, arid tension of this subjectivity is then interpreted as the
revolutionary spirit, the right fighting atmosphere. It appeals as the
apparent contrary to the condition of the hated bourgeois society – the
reverse of its luxuriant, materialistic confusion and vulgar egoism.
This rigorous neo-puritanism offers personal salvation, as well as the
promise of social revolution.

This and all the other traits of sectarian Marxism indicated – its
arrogance, its violent élitism, its instant and cutting condemnation of
all deviations from the 'line', its chronic substitution of insult for argument, its mystique of exclusive worker militancy, the cult of
organization – reflect the basic, precarious defensiveness of such movements. That is, its underlying historical task of conservatism, of
keeping alive the consciousness of revolution across the 'Hell-black
night' of the last decades. Naturally, it is wrong to assimilate this
species of conservatism to that of the Stalinist parties. It has different,
if related, causes and above all a different and historically valid motive.

---

*A. Gramsci, *Il Materialismo Storico*, pp. 13–15.
†The history of this syndrome, for instance, goes back as far as the founding
movement of the Trotskyite 'IVth International', in September 1938. Those critical of setting up such a body at this nadir of history were sternly rebuked by
the American delegate Schachtman for under-valuing the importance of organization. See December, *op. cit.*, pp. 419–22.

It is rather as if, precisely in being the historical 'anti-thesis' to Stalinism, the Marxist sects preserved in spite of themselves something of the fearful reality they were reacting against. They were compelled into an antithetical conservatism which, however inevitable, was almost as far removed from the reality and from the spirit of revolution.

Thus, it is much less surprising than appears at first sight that the 'groupuscules' were disconcerted and left behind by the revolutionary movement. The sudden rebirth of revolution, in such a startling different form, was bound to throw their contradictory nature into a relief almost as startling as that of the P.C.F. Naturally, the most 'open' groups (like the J.C.R.) had most influence and success; the most 'tough' or closed (like the O.C.I. and the F.E.R.) discredited themselves most completely. The Maoists (like the P.C.M.L.F.) were helped by the sheer irrelevance of their ideology to the problems of western society in general: paradoxically, this left them more free to create a revolutionary subjectivity.

The 'spontaneous' movement of revolt, so long awaited, had occurred not among the masses in the factories, but among the young intellectuals massed in the universities. They had become a directly-acting 'material' force of an unprecedented kind – an 'avant-garde' qualitatively different from the one envisaged by Leninism, larger, with a larger function, and a different relationship to society. The sects are currently clutching their tattered garments of doctrine to them, by maintaining that May was a revolution of the workers merely 'sparked off' by the 'heroic students'. To which one can only answer that this 'spark' was in fact a fire-storm, a high-temperature centre of revolution of a new kind. The pattern of revolution was almost reversed. Whereas Leninism envisaged capitalist society being prised up from below by a massive surge, which would then be transformed into an effective lever of revolution by the dynamic direction of the party – now society had split apart at the head, and the revolutionary contagion had spread out into the body in one devastating blow.

Within this extraordinary avalanche of action, the 'professional

revolutionaries' were defined by the revolution, instead of defining it.
A '22nd March' militant describes the main point in these terms:

> The importance of the event is obvious – guys who, if they tried
> talking about Marx, would be knocking each other's teeth out in
> five minutes, and screaming 'You bastard, you bloody counter-rev-
> olutionary' and all the rest of it – well, the same guys get on
> perfectly well when they have something definite to do together,
> like occupying an administration block, a precise task which just
> has to be done, or not done . . . the sort of task where one can say –
> 'If you are a revolutionary, do it; if you don't get on and do it then
> you're not a revolutionary. This *is* the revolution, it doesn't matter
> a damn what you think about Marx right now.'*

Within this process, the real truth that the sects stood for found a
place effortlessly, and the dogma was swept away on the tide along with
the other rubbish of the past. Thus, the exploding generosity of the revolutionary movement recognized without equivocation that it could
not develop beyond a certain point without the workers, that no revolution was possible which did not spread to the factories and rest,
finally, in the hands of the organized working class. But the blinkered
dogma of 'ouvrièrisme' – which had encapsulated this truth in the form
of diktat – simply faded away in the light of the facts.

The same causes explain the resurrection of anarchist thought and
feeling in May, the host of black flags which sprang up from nowhere
alongside the red ones. The anarchist 'groupuscules', feeble organiza-
tionally and small in numbers, were nevertheless far closer than the
Marxist sects to the spirit of what was happening –

> It was the anarchists who allowed the critique of Leninism to
> assume a concrete form, so that we could do things that were

Un Militant du 22 mars raconte, in the volume *Ce n'est qu'un début* (Edition
Spéciale, Editions et Publications Premières, 1968), pp. 56–7.

attacks on the university and the State, not just the Communist Party. They were the guarantors of democracy, they let everyone go on, the J.C.R., the Maoists, even the Young Communists. . . . So for instance if someone wanted to tell Danny 'You're an idiot', and go on telling him that for ten hours on end, he had the right to do just that. . . . They were the guarantee that while there was something to be done, people would drop their differences for the duration. . . . They were the ones who would say 'We can't wait light-years until all the objective conditions are there, let's do it now. . . . We can start the revolution now, here, at Nanterre.' Also they had the best ideas about daily living, about sex and so on, they let us get rid of all that consumer-society rubbish, and helped define a revolutionary moral code. Now, the 22nd March people are ready to get themselves killed for the revolution. . . . I don't consider myself an anarchist by the way.*

All the evidence of May suggests strongly that without a powerful dose of anarchic sentiment and ideas, a revolution of this sort and in these conditions is very unlikely to get far. It is no longer enough to say, with Lenin, that Marxists and anarchists can agree on distant aims – on the ultimate state of 'freedom' the revolution will one day bring about – but must disagree as to methods. Under advanced capitalism, where society is materially much closer to the possibility of 'freedom', means and ends are also necessarily much closer. Where release from bonds of alienation and authority is more important than bread, the immediate, violent voice of release is that much more important psychologically, and is more of a genuine lever of revolution than previously.

The important things about the action of May may have been forgotten, for so long, and for the reasons mentioned above. This is unimportant. In the light of the revolution, they are recovered easily, as people understand more in five minutes than they did in five, or fifty

*ibid., pp. 60–61.

years before. At the heart of the May revolution were the ancient things, found and lost and found again, in every past revolution worthy of that name. But more important still, in the centre of this truth, the new certainty in the bones of the students and young workers, that this time they will never, never be lost again. A humanity which has re-discovered its true height and image without being driven to the discovery by physical need has breached the last wall of pre-history. It will never crouch again beneath any fossilized tyranny, in the name of order, comfort, or an intangible future. To succeed, revolution has to be organized. But any organization which does not reflect this instinctive certainty completely is more likely to be a hindrance than a help.

F O U R

la chienlit, c'est lui

Even while the May revolutionary movement was in full spate, there was a widespread sense that its significance was universal. The London *Observer* warned its readers that:

> the events of the past three weeks are of historic importance. For they have crystallized longstanding, nagging doubts not only about France but about the nature of government in all advanced industrial societies – capitalist and communist alike. Something clearly is stirring under the surface of our inherited assumptions and conventional wisdom about the nature of our societies.*

However, the events were plainly very 'French', looked at from another angle. The question of what they mean for 'our' or other societies therefore depends upon a more precise understanding of their national character. Why did the May revolution occur in Paris, rather than anywhere else – rather than in Italy, for instance, where student revolt was more militant and on a larger scale? Do the local circumstances of its origin prevent one from considering it as a model for other times and places?

*Editorial, 26th May.

If the May revolt was libertarian in spirit, and aimed at a truly social control of society, then it is at least easy to see why, in the most general terms, it had to be revolutionary in character in France. Its 'local' characteristics, in this sense, flow from one fact: of all relevant and comparable nations, France was the one with least 'control' of any kind from below. It was almost totally deprived of living democracy. A recent American study of *The Paradoxes of the French Political Community* remarks constantly upon the near-absence of 'participation'.* It observes that France is the country where 'There is neither any real leadership or any real participation', that 'The transmission belts between nation and political régime are lacking', and that in France for some reason the 'synthesis between participation and authority' – difficult in any modern State – is almost non-existent.

Because the Fifth Republic was very much of a vacuum in this sense, clearly any resolute effort to grab some kind of 'participation' was more inherently explosive than elsewhere. After all, the vacuum was not mere absence or accident. It was the intended structure of the Fifth, without which the compensation for the void, the General, would not have agreed to emerge from the clouds again and assume power.

But this peculiar emptiness of the régime – felt as such even by the café-goers of the Champs-Elysées after the 24th of May, when it seemed that the revolution could occupy the void merely by reaching out to do so – was the logical counterpart of its success, on another level. And both sides of the contradiction were products of the past logic of French history.

The success of the Fifth Republic lay in its being, in so many ways, an admirable form of government for latter-day capitalism. Another irony of May is in this fact. Whatever archaic aspects persisted in the régime, it was also a model of enlightened, technocratic neo-capitalism – not at all a sick man of the capitalist world. Observers flocked to Paris to learn from this dynamic, intelligent system of administering the sheep. Capitalist rationalization, the strengthening and extension

*Stanley Hoffman, in *A la Recherche de la France* (Seuil, 1964).

of the power of the great monopolies, and the State-assisted adjustment
of the rest of the economy to suit them, was pursued with greater
verve and efficiency than in most other countries. The State power and
its technocratic administration was free to operate so dynamically just
because of the absence of 'transmission belts' connecting it to unwel-
come pressures and interests. The obvious contrast to France in this
regard is Britain. Here, governments struggled very hard for years to
achieve rejuvenatory results like those of de Gaulle's technocrats, and
their efforts came to nothing in the mire of British anti-rationalizing
muddle and pre-technocratic inertia.

This modern authoritarianism, at once so effective and so ultimately
disastrous in its repercussions, has deep roots in the history of France.
The celebrated opening of de Gaulle's *Memoirs* gives the great man's
own angle on this story –

> I am convinced that France is really herself only when she is in
> the front rank; only great enterprises can compensate for the dis-
> rupting ferment that her people carry in themselves. . . . Our
> country must, under pain of mortal danger, aim high and stand
> upright.

The 'disrupting ferment', which de Gaulle exploited so skilfully to re-
establish himself in power in 1958, is the never-healed conflict between
the political traditions of the revolution of 1789 and the predomi-
nantly anti-revolutionary reality of France. It was France which
produced the most perfect, the classical order of bourgeois political
democracy, thanks to the revolutionary energy of the Jacobin leadership of 1791 to 1795. But she proved thereafter chronically incapable
of making this order function properly. While the British Constitution,
that un-classical rag-bag of oddments, survived industrial revolution
and innumerable wars, the French Constitutions which succeeded one
another after the great revolution habitually collapsed at the slightest
crisis.

Perhaps the ultimate cause of this permanent contradiction may be

sought in the agrarian policy of the revolution itself, which turned the
countryside and small towns into permanent sources of anti-republican
reaction. Whatever the cause, the effects have been clear. As Jean-
François Revel has put it:

> Until very recently, French democrats made the mistake of think-
> ing that our authoritarian spirit and lack of any constitutional
> feeling were a passing illness, a kind of historical sediment that
> history would automatically eliminate. During the seventy years
> of the Third Republic (1871–1940) they believed that the French
> Revolution was the soul of France and the rest merely an acci-
> dental relic, a left-over from the past. Unfortunately these
> 'accidents' have been rather long-lived and repetitive – to the
> point where they must be considered as the normal reality of
> France. It is time to look facts in the face and admit that the
> French Revolution has definitely lost the fight. . . .*

To the revolutionary and democratic tradition of 1789, 1830, 1848
and 1871, one must oppose the hideous *série noire* of Napoléon, the
Restoration, Napoléon III, Boulanger, Pétain, and de Gaulle, and admit
that the latter have ruled most of the time, and not by accident. Even
the one long spell of parliamentary democracy enjoyed by France was
precarious, and has been described as –

> An epoch in which the idea of democracy was never quite secure,
> and the idea of reaction never quite dared openly to organize itself
> as a party seeking to overthrow democratic foundations.†

What continuity there is – if any – between the old revolutionary tradition and May must be established. Until May, it looked as if the old
conflict had been resolved for good with the definitive triumph of the

---

*J-F. Revel, *Contrecensures* (1966), p. 60.
†H. J. Laski, preface to *France is a Democracy*, by L. Lévy (1943).

authoritarian spirit in the farce of May, 1958. Ten years ago, a military rebellion in Algiers was the pretext for the final guillotining of the traditions of 1789. The lack of faith in the Fourth of the French Republics was so deep that this squalid revolt of colonial die-hards and embittered colonels – which came no nearer the French mainland than Corsica – was felt as a mortal threat. Democracy crumbled away in a welter of plot and counter-plot. De Gaulle was then able to present himself as the 'only alternative' to a *coup* by the extreme right and a fascist régime. The Republic then collapsed into his arms. Guy Mollet, leader of the social-democratic S.F.I.O. party, who on 28th May, 1958 marched in the front rank of the giant procession 'in defence of the Republic' (where one of the most popular slogans was '*De Gaulle au Musée*'), crawled to Colombey-les-Deux-Églises on the 30th. He returned in the finest revolutionary tradition, confessing that

> This has been one of the great days in my life. . . . Even the Communists should be voting for him now. . . . De Gaulle has become a true republican.*

Within two days, de Gaulle was in power. This miserable end to the great work of *l'An II* is only explicable in terms of an almost total public disillusionment with the apparatus of bourgeois democracy. As a leading expert in the decipherment of the constitutional mysteries of the Fifth Republic indicates, regarding the origins of the monster –

> There may be doubts regarding the real strength of the movement that threatened France with a *coup d'état*. There can be none regarding the real weakness of the Republican will to resist. . . . The predominant atmosphere in France was one of political

---

*Mai 1958, in Le Monde (22nd May–5th June, 1968), by Pierre Viansson-Ponté. Le Monde chose this appropriate moment to publish a history of the 'events' of ten years before, and so remind its readers of the true nature of the régime now defending 'democracy' and 'the Republic' with such energy.

apathy . . . of growing disrespect for Parliament and for politicians
on the part of the public.*

The ensuing régime was baptized the Fifth Republic, instead of the
Fifth Empire, because de Gaulle was more cunning than his predecessors in the profession. He saw the need to erect a republican façade
around his personal rule. This was to be a 'constitutional dictatorship'
which would reconcile the conflicting elements of the disrupting ferment. It would satisfy the nation's real, underlying desire for a strong
hand at the helm – but also its periodic delusions of democracy, and
the insatiable vanity of the Tricolour tradition.

The political vacuum which was certainly one of the conditions of
the May explosion is not therefore just an aspect of Gaullism: it was a
precondition of the régime. It suits the General and his minions to
rattle the bones of bourgeois democracy, when they are threatened. But
neither they nor any Sixth Republic will put the flesh back on them. In
France, parliamentarism has become a relic, a skeleton of use only to
the counter-revolution. Its true role in the Fifth is described in the most
incisive survey of the past decade, in these terms:

> In June 1964, I recall seeing our Minister of Finance and
> Economic Affairs rise to speak at the Assemblée Nationale, in the
> course of one of its rare meetings, those painful caricatures of
> parliamentary debate whose only point is to give the govern-
> ment a chance of heaping insult after insult on the heads of an
> inexistent opposition. . . . The Minister was to pronounce on the
> Meat Problem, since – in spite of the much-vaunted 'price-sta-
> blization plan' – meat persisted in costing more and more each
> day. Two or three representatives of the 'Opposition' said as
> much, timorously and without conviction (I suspect that lots
> had been drawn to decide who the day's victims should be).
> Upon which, the Minister rose up in all his wrath to declare that

*Dorothy Pickles, *The Fifth French Republic* (3rd edition 1965), pp. 15–17.

it was 'inadmissible' to 'joke' about a rise of a 'few centimes' when
the entire responsibility for the rise clearly lay with the Fourth
Republic. Had not the régime inflicted bad 'structures' on the
meat business? (Under the Fifth, Ministers are 'structuralists'
like everybody else.) I must confess to a certain admiration for
the man. The Fifth had held absolute power for close on seven
years, yet it was still possible for him to go on attributing the
most trivial mishaps to the Fourth, without the whole nation
collapsing in one enormous fit of laughter.*

This may help to explain why the May demonstrations largely
ignored the Assemblée Nationale. The Second Empire was overthrown
in 1870 to the accompaniment of a dramatic invasion of parliament
and the proclamation of a new régime. In 1968, this would have been
a waste of time: parliamentarism reached the point of no return in the
1958 fiasco, and can probably never be revived in anything like its old
form.

We noticed already in what sense a revolutionary action like May is
the reversal of the prevailing socio-economic categories. In France,
the political void, the inability of the system to offer even a plausible
façade of old-style 'democracy' which could channel the movement,
gives enormous resonance to its directness. It is at once evident that
real dissent must start from the very bottom, from outside the system,
from the streets, the schools, the factories. Because the traditional
apparatus of indirect control, elections, assemblies, and so on, is seen
as dupery it is taken for granted that meaningful action is direct, that
representatives are untrustworthy, and that 'politics' is – everywhere,
and everything. Power must be simple: the opposite of de Gaulle's
mystification and the complexity of the technocracy, the collective
seizure and control of whatever matters most.

While most other western régimes furnish subjects with – at least –
certain illusions of participation, the French have enjoyed a substitute

*J-F. Revel. *En France* (1965), pp. 65–6.

since 1958. They had chosen another version of the perennial consolation of their past: identification with a 'great man'. This great man had more of the ideal Saviour's qualities than any of his predecessors: a General (the National Soul always wears a uniform), a man of fewer words (fortunately) than Napoléon III, infinitely cleverer than Pétain, and already a hall-marked redeemer from the *débâcle* of 1940. What 'participation' can he now offer France that could possibly equal that participation in his own narcissistic identity of the Nation and himself which the country has gone through in the last ten years?

De Gaulle's vulgar archaism has often confused observers. Alexander Werth says in his study of the man:

> I (once) described de Gaulle as 'a noble anachronism'; and at that time it seemed true. In a sense it is still true; for there is a genuine touch of melancholy in de Gaulle's recent remark: 'Ah, *cher ami*, if only we were a nation of 180 million people!' But I am prepared to eat my 1956 words. For in the last few years, de Gaulle has shown that even if he is a 'man of yesterday', he is also a 'man of tomorrow'.*

This being a man of tomorrow, Werth adds, in his capacity to rule a 'thoroughly modern and efficient State' and to 'move with the times'.

But there is historical sense in this contrast between the anachronism and the modern economy it presides over. If we try to trace this sense, we may arrive at a fuller vision of the particular contradictions that produced the revolution. We have seen the political relationship between the revolution and the 'vacuum' of the Fifth; and how the latter was the result of the régime's political effort to reconcile historical conflicts. But these political relations, in turn, only find their real meaning within a deeper context.

The reason for the persisting, unresolved conflict between a reactionary authoritarianism and the ideas of 1789 in French history is to

---

*A. Werth, *De Gaulle* (Penguin Books, 1965), p. 57.

be sought in its second-rate capitalist development. That is, in the weakness that made France the 'bourgeois' country *par excellence*, but not the capitalist one. A certain weakness of development stemmed from the Revolution itself, which was essentially political in nature, not economic (like the English industrial revolution proceeding at the same time), and bought its political success by compromise with rural backwardness. Later, domestic capitalist growth was further distorted – as in Britain – by the influence of imperialism, which diverted capital to investment in Eastern Europe and Africa, and led to the formation of a large *rentier* class. It was in the resultant comfortable stagnation that the central antagonism could endure for so long. That vegetative *douceur de vivre*, so characteristic of the Third Republic and so inimical to the strenuous virtues of capital-accumulation, was also the condition of continuing backwardness and authoritarianism.

The mission of the Fifth was to end all this. It was to put France on her feet again, after the collapse of her imperialism, by restoring her into the mainstream of capitalist development. It was to employ all the formidable resources of the highly centralized French State administration to this economic end, with greater force and decision than an old-fashioned bourgeois Republic could. Thus, as well as reconciling the old conflicts in its political form, it would also remove their festering source in a tide of socio-economic modernization.

De Gaulle's function was to be the midwife of the change. His efficacy derived, precisely, from his not being a 'man of tomorrow'. The men of today and tomorrow are singularly lacking in the charisma that might enable them to command such dramatic transformations, as a glance around the European political scene will show. Modern bourgeois society no longer produces such creatures: it produces ghosts, in its own image. Like the last other 'great man' of Europe, Churchill, de Gaulle's power over the present comes from a certain imaginative density, a residue of romanticism, a large and irrational individualism which is the very contrary of what the technocracy stands for. The leverage such men have held over society shows more clearly than anything else the drab mediocrity, the human feebleness of European neo-capitalism.

Turning again to look at the reality of this society in the fierce light of May, Edgar Morin saw how the events had thrown into relief

> . . . the drama of modern bourgeois society, so-called 'industrial society'. The old traditional values that moulded bourgeois society up to the present are progressively eaten away by an economistic dynamic and the concentration of values on private individualism, that is – as far as everything outside such individualism is concerned – on nihilism. . . . This results finally in an extraordinarily soft, protoplasmic social reality . . . a society with a very weak sense of community, an almost inorganic aggregate of individuals that crumbles at the first shock.*

This society is, by nature, totally lacking in magic. The apotheosis of capitalism is also the lived revelation of the inward barrenness of the system, whose only 'magic' is in fact the private satisfactions of the consumer myth. If 'affluence' ceases for one half-instant to be everything, then it is nothing. The world of scarcity's millennial dream, realized in capitalist conditions, turns out to be the thinnest of paper screens, a lantern-slide image which dissolves at a touch.

In France, an archaic power was the midwife of neo-capitalist society, because no other could be. Only an incarnation of past magic could conjure up the future. Rationalization could only be conducted by a dusty, antiquated lie straight out of nineteenth-century history books. The impersonal, Europeanized society-to-be could only be forced on in a nauseating tide of renewed chauvinism, in the putrescent jingoism of the Fifth Republic.

Hence, the Fifth was necessarily a bizarre clash of past and present, whose 'structure' was a lie. In social reality, France saw the neo-capitalist 'economic miracle', the onrush of an aggressive, individualistic

*E. Morin, *Une Révolution sans visage*, op. cit.

materialism in its most brutal forms. Cultified in the French mystique of 'technique' (the simplest way of saying that, here too, the French are superior to everyone else), this development was all the more vicious and naked for contrasting so markedly with the ancient French bourgeois style of living. It was as if the placid old individualism, with its enclosed cultivation of the good life, had flowered into violent, carnivorous form in the forcing-house of Gaullism. The open wounds of these contrasts made France the most unlivable corner of the western world, when for so long it had been the most comfortable. The dead, authoritarian void became an abrasive place of encounter where the old nationalistic fetishism and the new commodity-fetishism jostled together, where *joie de vivre* gave way to sour aggressiveness, and *vieille France* became a more and more remote escape-route from this odious reality.*

We saw why, in the empty *dépolitisation* of Gaullism, genuine political action had to invent its own simple and elementary forms, a new reality untainted by past or present. The social and economic conflicts that correspond to the void explain why such invention was likely to be violent, and extremely contagious. The gunpowder was surely the

*Jean-Luc Godard's film *Weekend* (1967) has been widely interpreted as a prophetic vision of May 1968. It is a story of a week-end escape to a countryside where the rustic bliss has been destroyed by tourist-eating rebels, blazing cars, and corpses. But this is over-simple. The film is certainly a powerful depiction of the *violence* of Gaullist France, incarnated in its advert-photo characters ('*jeunes cadres*') and their degenerate obsessions. Their non-humanity is conveyed by their indifference to the bloody corpses strewing the countryside and the casualness with which one slits his mother's throat to get an inheritance. But this very effective *guignol* contrasts strikingly (and characteristically) with the film's failure of imagination on the main point, the young rebels. The *Front de Libération de la Seine-et-Oise*, far from anticipating the liberating violence of May ('counter-violence'), practises a bestial violence which is the extreme form of the conventional aggressiveness shown earlier. The effect is therefore to *épater* the bourgeoisie in a conventional way, rather than to escape imaginatively from its categories.

particularly overt 'human crisis' of the Fifth Republic (in Morin's phrase), the flayed nerves of a society too openly exposed to the contradictions of the most advanced capitalism.

A certain 'apathy' is the normal protection against these contradictions, the hide which is grown to remain whole. This is of course the customary state of student bodies, before they are touched by revolt. Time and time again, it has been seen how rapidly such protection vanishes whenever a sense of collective being and potential is generated, how miraculous powers of action and expression surge out almost at once. The real wealth created by society lies hidden a membrane's distance away, under modern conditions, waiting to live in a revolutionary situation or die invisible if the membrane is never pierced. In France, apathy had to assume the particularly egoistic and aggressive forms mentioned because the tensions were so much more powerful. The reaction and release were therefore more extreme. France was the country of lies: the new horrors of Europeanization in conflict with the old, comfortable bourgeois lies of the nineteenth century; all wrapped in the fetid, dishonoured flag of French nationalism and finding no possibility of political relief under the lie of 'personal rule', a dictatorship all the more effective for being able to dispense with the crudities of Hitler and Mussolini. Everyone recognizes that there was no 'economic crisis' in the usual sense behind the May revolt, that as one writer has put it –

> France was in good form, that is, she was getting on very happily with her cancer in the calm certainty that it would never strike her dead . . .*

The point is, in fact, that economic well-being merely aggravates *this* kind of 'cancer'. A period of boom is more likely to be fatal than a conventional 'crisis'.

But as well as the lies, the Fifth Republic also inherited a by-product

*Claude Lefort, *Le Désordre Nouveau*, in *La Brèche: Mai 1968*, p. 39.

of the historical dissensions the régime intended to heal up. This was
the sharper, more articulate political consciousness associated with
them. Even although – in the nature of things in France – the revolutionary tradition was a tradition of *rhetoric* largely, nevertheless this
provided at least a framework within which a universalizing consciousness of these new contradictions could appear quickly, once
dépolitisation was broken through. The Fifth Republic had neither the
time, nor the ideological resources, to bury this inheritance deeply
enough under the mystifications required to maintain anaesthesia and
immobility in contemporary society. It was, therefore, especially vulnerable to the new contradictions within the forces of 'mental
production' (mentioned in the next chapter).

It is clear from such considerations that France and her Fifth
Republic were more than a mere local habitation and name for the
Revolution of May. There are many precise and pressing reasons which
made it break out there rather than in another place, and conferred its
particular character on it. Is there not consequently some conflict
between such a 'particular', contingent situation and the Universal
Significance so easily read into it since May? Why should this be seen
as *the* revolution, rather than as another and entirely French revolution?

In part, the answer to this question must be that the French
'extremes' operative in preparing the revolution were just that. Every
major factor in it can be found in every other country that France can
reasonably be compared with.

Is the decline of parliamentary democracy peculiar to France? On
the contrary, it is common to Western Europe, and a topic of anxious
debate currently even in England ('Mother of Parliament'). It was
merely put to its severest test in France, where the decay became collapse in 1958. Is technocratic capitalism a particularly French
phenomenon? Not at all, the same general tendencies and problems are
found everywhere, disguised and cushioned in various ways by a vari-
ety of traditional forces. Is the nihilistic individualism described by
Morin specifically French? It can be found in Birmingham or Turin or

Frankfurt equally well, in forms not yet quite as corrosive. Are the new problems of higher education and student revolt confined to France? Of course not, they are universal and – as we saw – were more evolved than in France until May. The underlying class-contradiction whose antagonism was set in motion again with greater virulence by the May events is not French – in many other countries, it is more acute and far less disciplined.

True, other countries have no de Gaulle. But he is merely the last turn of the screw, and each country must give its own highly individual form to that. In England, for instance, the finale of parliamentarism would never be a vulgar personal dictatorship, for the Westminster fetish could never be given up. It could only be a permanent coalition or 'national Government' summing up the glorious past in the same way as de Gaulle and with the same general policies.

Hence, the May revolution was 'typical', in the sense of exposing forces which were in extreme form and contradiction, but are present everywhere. However, there is more to the specificity than this allows for. The May revolution was 'universal' in a much more vital sense, a sense inseparable from the specificity or 'Frenchness' of the event. In fact, its universality *is* its 'local character', in a way that could not possibly have been true anywhere else. It is *because* the revolution broke out in France first, and could not have done so elsewhere – because it was entirely 'local', therefore – that it is entirely universal in its significance.

The explanation of this paradox is found in the *diagrammatic* or symbolic character of the revolution. This is precisely the thing which is entirely 'French', because of French articulacy, because of the highly developed rhetoric of the revolutionary tradition, because of the extraordinarily high pitch of *consciousness* attained by the revolutionary movement in a short time and with the least material change. And yet, of course, *this* local colour is also by its very nature universal.

In May, as perhaps never before in history, actions were words, and words actions, in a 'real-life drama' of meanings. One must recognize in this the truly French *grandeur*, the giant historical character beside

which de Gaulle and the tawdry chest-beating of the Fifth Republic
dwindle to dust. It is possible to ask whether things like the May
upheaval could have 'happened' somewhere else. But it is not possible
to doubt that the sense of the 'happening' could never have been *shown*
anywhere else, with this incomparable clarity and generosity, so that
the showing *was* the happening.

Naturally, this is also the respect in which May 1968 re-echoes and
prolongs the great revolutionary tradition of the past. All revolutions
rise to such heights momentarily, in the heat of their forward movement. But it is more important to see that May, 1968, also *transcends*
this tradition in a quite fundamental respect.

The French-revolutionary inheritance is one of *political* revolts, of
radical and conscious transformations of the social 'superstructure'.
And Marx pointed out that this was a defect, as well as a virtue. The
'over-politicization' of the French revolutionaries led them to purchase
their success originally at too high a social and economic cost, in a
society not yet ripe for the change. Later, it led them to attempt revolutions (1848, 1871) doomed to defeat because of the impossibly large
discrepancy between political and ideological awareness and what
social reality was capable of. Political revolution had become an obsession, its traditions had become partially mystifying – as was proved, he
thought, in the culminating disaster of the 1871 Paris Commune.

In one sense, perhaps, May 1968 may be seen as continuing the tradition of a rhetoric which tries boldly to advance upon reality, an
ideological willpower confident in its power over things. The rhetori-
cal, 'exemplary' nature of the revolution was also its precocity, and its
necessary weakness. However, this cleavage between idea and reality in
no way recalls the distorting and fatal contradiction of the past. The
latter was caused by a recalcitrance of social reality in the face of the
idea, for which there was no historical remedy but the defeat of the
idea, in the shorter or the longer term. In 1968, on the contrary, the
discrepancy was simply the shock, the utter surprise and novelty of the
revolutionary conjuncture.

And in the lightning-flash the 'reality' appeared as overwhelmingly 'ripe' for the 'idea', though its movement forward scarcely had time to begin, and remained therefore a diagrammatic sketch of revolution like all the actions of May. In its essential structure, the embryonic revolution of 1968 appeared to have gone beyond the main historical weakness of the great tradition to which it belongs. It is, therefore, not a faint re-echo of the past, not the dim memory of Jacobinism dressed up in the garments of a contemporary charade, not in any way a 'pseudo-revolution' where history repeats itself as a joke. It is the early manifestation of a revolutionary process much greater than those of the past. Every past revolution has been 'wrong', in the sense of being in a discord with the real potential of society, at that historical moment: 1640, 1789, the revolutions of the nineteenth century, and of course the socialist revolutions in backward countries of this century. May, 1968 was the precursor of the first revolution in history which can be 'right', where the collective human voice can at last utter the immense, gathered potential of human culture where it presses invisibly upon the frame of the archaic social order. Because it is – in a sense to be established – 'overdue' as no other historical revolt was or could be, it is sure of a success and a meaning which no other revolt could have. Whereas all other revolutions were inevitably struggles against impossible odds, where a great deal of the revolutionary vision was certain to be lost ('betrayed', even after the immediate political triumph of the movement) the new revolution will – on the contrary – exceed every vision, break every obstacle, and realize the dreams of maturity, of which we are as yet scarcely conscious.*

*The bankruptcy of society before the revolutionary challenge of May is shown as clearly by de Gaulle's reaction as anything else. No *alternative* is possible – only a deformed caricature of what the revolution itself prefigures: the new programme of State-guided 'participation', which is supposed to trace a middle course between capitalism and communism. The nature of Gaullist participation was clear enough in the speech of 7th June: 'Participation . . . has always been the right road, as far as I am concerned. . . . Discussion in common, followed by the action of one man by himself. This will be the character of participation as of all other sorts of behaviour.'

FIVE

new contradictions

All these other questions return one insistently to the central one: what had changed in the heart of social reality, to make what was inconceivable yesterday into a matter of fact? The unpredictability of the phenomenon, the dramatic opening of what Sartre called 'the horizons of the possible' in May, the profound novelties thrown up almost casually by the movement on every hand – everything suggests that if society has secretly transformed itself to make such originality possible, then this transformation must be of the utmost importance, must represent a turning-point second to none in the development of human history.

The proximate, visible cause of the upheaval lay in the student revolt, in the universities. That is, in society's 'higher nervous system', in a rebellion of the higher 'nerve centres'. Pursuing the metaphor then, one must ask what is the new nature of this system, capable of generating rebellion on such a scale. We saw already that it can scarcely be coincidence that the first 'perfect' generation produced by capitalism is like this – but what is the machinery of the comedy? And – still more important – what is the new relationship between the 'nervous system' and the whole social body, which allows the former to be the initiator of revolution?

These 'nerve-centres' of western society, the institutions of higher education and particularly the universities, have obviously changed very greatly in the last half-century, in a way that constantly crops up in every diagnosis of student revolt. They are enormously larger, and have a different and larger significance for society. They are now the products of an 'academic revolution' which has transformed them from their old function, the formation of a narrow and privileged élite of social administrators, to a new one. Today, they train a far larger number of intellectual specialists of all sorts, more widely diffused throughout the social body. The old university produced what Gramsci called 'traditional intellectuals' (writers, men of letters, teachers, clergy, professional men and social administrators who belonged to the same culture-world). The new university, as well as a much greater number of these, and their modern successors (e.g. journalists, media-men), also produces a great number of what he called 'organic intellectuals' more closely and necessarily related to the economic structure (e.g., technicians, managers, ad-men, and so on).

This 'academic revolution' is in turn the product of something else. That is, of the immense growth in the productive forces of western society during the same period. The creation of 'intellectuals' on a scale so much greater than in the past is the sign that this growth is not simply a growth in quantity, but contains a qualitative change within itself. The crisis among these 'intellectuals', then, differs in essential nature from previous intellectual disturbances to the extent to which it embodies this change. It is the sign that the change is not a linear progress, but a dialectical development containing contradictions of its own, not reducible to the older social categories, and only now beginning to display their real character. As a commentator on the American academic revolution (in many ways more advanced than the European) puts it:

> It may be true that the more advanced social systems of our own
> era may well be caught up in unprecedented dialectical conflicts
> of their own that threaten their internal stability. Societies consist

not of classes and institutions only, but of the human beings who
give them substance: if institutions systematically frustrate the
needs and aspirations of considerable numbers of their ablest and
most valuable functionaries, then a quasi-Marxian analysis may
still be appropriate. To my knowledge, no one has disproved such
a possibility in the circumstances that concern us here.*

The 'unprecedented dialectical conflict' exposed in May in the form
of revolution can only be understood in terms of this underlying
change of equilibrium. That is, in terms of a mutation which gives us
the proper criterion of what constitutes the 'maturity' of capitalist-
industrial society. Revolution could not come before maturity, and
maturity is the phase in which the forces of material production – the
mainspring of all historical change so far – have brought about a decisive development in the *forces of mental production*.

The development of these forces assumes two closely-related forms,
corresponding to the 'traditional' and 'organic' categories mentioned
above. One is associated with the major growth in the old élite of ide-
ologists and administrators deriving from the swelling complexity of
contemporary society and its prodigious and ever-increasing apparatus
of *communication*: the 'mass media', 'popular' culture, and the transformation of the conscious environment these have brought about.
The other is rooted more directly in the development of industrial and
administrative technology, and consists of the specialized intellectual
skills the process requires: its great symbol is the computer, the high-
est form of technical intelligence, and its tendency is to transform an
ever-larger sector of the economy – along with the cities which house
economic organization, and the State which services it – into the pro-
cessing of *information* (the 'information revolution').

Thus, an ever-greater part of the modern economy and of social life
generally is given over to the production of *consciousness*. But this
entire development sprang necessarily from within the forces of mate-

*H. D. Aitken, *The Revolting Academy*, in the *New York Review*, 11th July, 1968.

rial production, from the industrial production and the commercial
distribution of *things*, 'commodities'. It is the ultimate triumph of the
latter, in post-war American and European capitalism, which has precipitated the former forward at such a rate. 'Advanced' capitalism, or
'consumer capitalism', the definitive victory of materialism in a universal worship of the commodity-fetish, is impossible without the mass
media, advertising, and automation, without a parallel expansion of the
social 'brain' and the nerves of communication. Naturally, in western
society such evolution is harnessed to commodity-production – the
increasing powers of mental production are subordinated to the dom-
inating powers of material production and circumscribed within its
categories. But it does not follow that this subordination is the whole
truth of the historical situation, as so many have assumed.

It has always been recognized that humanity will become 'free' and
adult, to the extent to which it transcends the necessities of material
production. That is, when it leaves behind the millennial effort of labo-
riously transforming the environment, and can finally stand upright on
this secure material basis and cultivate its own intrinsic, human potential. Such cultivation must evidently take the form of 'culture', the
enormous development of social consciousness, and consequent
enrichment of everyone's individual experience.

According to Marx's conception of man's advance towards this condition, capitalism will necessarily be the ultimate stage of the
development of the forces of material production. The prodigious
magic of Capital will unfold, carrying men farther in a few years than
in all the past millennia, to the edge of freedom. Only when this edge
is reached, when the colossal apparatus of commodity-production has
unfolded 'fully', will it permit liberation from its own alienation. It will
then be transcended by a revolutionary process. There is a graphic
account of this 'mature' state in the *Grundrisse*:

The great historic role of Capital is the creation of surplus labour,
labour which is superfluous from the standpoint of mere use
value, mere subsistence. This historical function is fulfilled when,

on the one hand, needs have been developed to the point where such surplus labour . . . has itself become a general need which is expressed in the needs of individual people, and – on the other hand – when the strict discipline of Capital has schooled successive generations in industriousness, and this quality has become a common inheritance, and when (finally) the productive powers of labour, constantly spurred on by Capital in its limitless drive towards accumulation, have ripened to the point where the maintenance of social wealth requires no more than a very limited amount of labour-time, and where scientific processes regulate the reproduction and growth of this wealth towards ever greater abundance. In other words, where a reified, machine-like human labour has ceased altogether.*

However, 'reification' (the form in which capitalism persists, even in maturity) will only vanish on the other side of the revolutionary transition. Later on, Marx points out that such a capitalist 'affluent society' where automation plays an increasing part in production, itself negates many conventional capitalist categories. It renders absurd the estimation of value in terms of old-fashioned individual 'labour-time', since the power of labour is so many times magnified by automation, and what is really being harnessed is the 'collective productive power' of society, its intelligence of nature and consequent ability to dominate it. The social nature of production becomes more important, and more evident. Things begin to appear as they really are, through the fragmentation and mystification of the system –

Nature does not build machines . . . these are the products of human industry, of natural materials turned into instruments of human will and activity . . . They are instruments of the human

---

*Grundrisse der Kritik der politischen Okonomie (Rohentwurf), Berlin 1953, p. 231; French translation, Fondements de la Critique de l'Economie Politique (Editions Anthropos, Paris 1967), vol. 1, p. 273. Author's translation.

brain, created by the hand of man, the materialized organs of his knowledge.*

The conflict between the social nature of production and the endless series of alienating splits which bourgeois society inflicts upon it (between the worker and his tools, between the worker and the product of his work, between one unit of production and another, etc., etc.) therefore comes to a head in capitalism's maturity. The 'social' becomes embodied in the 'brain', in the social intelligence, the knowledge that increasingly 'regulates the reproduction and growth of wealth'.

The last phase of Capital's progress, hence, does more than simply establish the 'material conditions' for liberation (in the sense of relief from primary poverty, the development of productive forces to the stage where some kind of socialism is 'materially possible'). It also *anticipates* the future state of society, beyond the revolution, in its *form* – in the *real* organization of production within the persisting (or even intensified) alienation of the system (its chronic 'mis-organization'). Evidently, there must be an essential contradiction operative here, peculiar to the later stages of the system. And it would be surprising indeed if it could be reduced to the terms of those older contradictions previously generated within capitalism (the contradictions of 'immature', evolving bourgeois society, still preserved in the unfolded system).

It would be no less surprising if Marx had been able to foresee the nature of this contradiction fully. In fact, the new conflict – which is also the ultimate conflict of the bourgeois social order, in the double sense of being last in time, and such that it can never be resolved inside the system – is rooted in the great development of the forces of mental production, in a multitude of forms whose character and effect were only dimly visible until much more recently. One way of indicating the nature, and novelty, of the change is perhaps to say that the

Grundrisse, pp. 593–4; *Fondements*, vol. 2, pp. 221–3.

central contradictions of later capitalism are focused in what would traditionally have been called the social 'superstructure' (because they
involve social consciousness and ideology, and the quintessentially
'superstructural' institution of the university). But they cannot really be
opposed to the contradictions or problems of the socio-economic
'structure' (i.e. the apparatus of material production, and the form it
takes in existing society) because they evidently derive from it. The
material forces of production in western capitalism would not sustain
themselves or advance one half-centimetre farther without the continued operation and expansion of this 'superstructure' – without the *real*
activity of the 'intellectuals', both organic and traditional, and the constantly growing importance of their function. Late capitalist society is
infinitely more *united* than the conventional categories allow for, and
this unity (because the system remains divisive at the same time) is
itself an omnipresent contradiction.

Perhaps the sense of the contradiction may be clearer if one recalls
the past history of society's powers of mental production. These powers
are in essence identical with the distinctively human or 'social' structure. This social structure (which distinguishes human from all animal
'societies') is a dialectical and inherently contradictory one between the
individual and the social group he belongs to materially. This relationship of individual and group is the extremely developed
communicative one of *language*. Through this communication-net-
work of various linguistic codes, the collective consciousness of the
'social' group is created, and continuously reproduced within the individual (so that each individual carries 'society' around within his skull,
internalized through language). In one sense therefore, the linguistic
relationship characterizing 'society' looks like a complicated form of
subordination of the individual awareness to society, a form of social
control.

But the inner contradiction of the relationship – which explains
both the immense superiority of human society to any other gregar-
ious form imaginable, and the instability that is inseparable from it –
lies in the necessary development of individual potential which its

working entails. For a communication-system to work as the arma-
ture of a group, individual communicative power must be developed,
as individual consciousness potentially distinct from that expressed
in the codes. To 'understand' *is* to speak, in linguistic terms, to speak
is to internalize the code as an individual reality: to 'speak to oneself'
or think. Hence, society in constantly re-creating itself within the
individual also constantly *loses itself* in the individual. The 'subordination' of the individual, mediated in this fashion, is also potentially
at every instant the loss of society within the individual, the subordination of society to an individual consciousness (and therefore to
more than one such consciousness, since the code is precisely a social
phenomenon of diffusion). The 'individual' awareness, in 'personal'
speech or thought, is nothing without the social communication-
code; but the code or language is itself nothing but so many
individual 'expressions', so many acts of speech. This is the sense in
which man is a 'species-being' according to Marx's definition in the
1844 Manuscripts: 'he' (the individual) *is* the network of socio-lin-
guistic relationships around him, and it *is* him and the other
individuals who embody it.

Human 'history' is founded upon this dynamic of interaction, the
living dialectic which haunts every moment of human consciousness.
This, rather than the tool, is the lever which tears men out of nature
(for material instruments can only be developed and transmitted in a
context of language). But the history that is the development of this
potential – the 'powers of mental production' which are the essence of
society – is also, necessarily, the negation of it, the repression and dis-
tortion of its true meaning.

In primitive society, first of all, it is trapped within the dense conservatism marking the group's struggle against the overwhelming
pressure of the natural environment. Then in the history of 'civilization' that follows, it is harnessed to the secular task of transforming
this environment – to the slow development of the material forces of
production. Because history is material, in this sense, consciousness
is subordinated to its needs in the form of the classical division

between 'mental' and 'manual' labour. The consciousness of the social body is canalized into a small governing élite that presides over the slavery of the majority, forced into the apparatus of material production. Because the latter is more important historically, the mental domination of the former takes the form of 'ideology', a *false* consciousness of control and coercion unconsciously rooted in material production.

The successful 'conquest of the environment', the development of material production to the point where scarcity is eliminated, obviously means the release of the social 'essence' – of the intrinsic 'idealism' of human existence from the half-human compulsions of matter. Western capitalism is now on the threshold of this condition, it is possible at least to foresee it. But hitherto, this has been seen as the final material state of civilization: the last plateau of material abundance (which must be transcended, still, out of material causes – because of the contradictions built into alienated material production). In fact, though (as we saw), this phase of history is also a prefiguration of the future in its *form* – because of the ripening development of the 'social' inside it, in the shape of collective intelligence and consciousness.

The transition from primitive society to civilization was made possible by the slow creation and use of a *material surplus* – the amount over and above what was necessary for social survival. The transition from civilization to communism, in turn, is made possible by the creation of a 'mental surplus' – that is, by the development of mental production to the point where it exceeds the demands of the material matrix. This, rather than the tensions inherent in the matrix of material production, becomes the directly 'revolutionary' agent which will finally compel the transformation. Capitalism generated this revolutionary agent to serve itself, it produced education and the exploding communication and information systems in order to intensify its own material growth, as capital-accumulation. Now, however, these forces are turning into apprentice-sorcerers, undermining the whole reified structure of accumulation. The ultimate phase of capitalist productivity, in other words, is the mass-production of consciousness as a commodity. But consciousness resists the form of commodity-production, by its very dialectical and social character.

This contradiction is clearly manifested in the two principal positions taken up by theorists who have considered the problem. One arm of it is represented, for instance, by T. W. Adorno, who sees the influence of 'mass culture' as –

> Regimentation, the result of the progressive societalization of all human relations . . . (which) . . . imposes itself as relentlessly on the autonomous mind as heteronomous orders were formerly imposed on the mind which was bound. Not only does the mind mould itself for the sake of its marketability, and thus reproduce the socially prevalent categories. Rather, it grows to resemble ever more closely the *status quo* even where it subjectively refrains from making a commodity of itself. The network of the whole is drawn ever tighter, modelled after the act of exchange. It leaves the individual consciousness less and less room for evasion, preforms it more and more thoroughly . . . (hence) . . . the regression of spirit and intellect. In accordance with the predominant social tendency, the integrity of the mind becomes a fiction.*

Hence, the system is being *entirely successful* in tying the development of culture down to the old, alienated basis. The mass consciousness generated by the new means of production is even more the slave of the 'socially prevalent categories' than before – it is either crystallized directly within these categories, or else indirectly, as a 'drug' or an escape-route to a 'leisure' whose whole purpose is the recreation of labour energy.

On the other hand, there is the strikingly contrasted thesis asso-

---

*T. W. Adorno, *Prisms* (trans. S. W. Weber, 1967), p. 21. See also *L'Industrie culturelle*, by the same author, in No. 3 of the review *Communications* (Ecole Pratique des Hautes Études, Paris).

ciated with, for instance, Marshall McLuhan and his school. They see the growth of modern communications as in itself a revolutionary liberation of – and a qualitative change in – social consciousness. The new powers of mental production contained in our 'electric technology' release us from the 'mechanical patterns' of the past, so that –

> The aspiration of our time for wholeness, empathy and depth of awareness is a natural adjunct of electric technology. The age of mechanical industry that preceded us found vehement assertion of private outlook the natural mode of expression. Every culture and every age has its favourite model of perception and knowl-edge that it is inclined to prescribe for everybody and everything. The mark of our time is its revulsion against imposed patterns. We are suddenly eager to have things and people declare their beings totally . . .*

Far from imprisoning us still more completely and subtly, therefore, this culture is the implicit negation of the imprisoning categories. As a consequence of automation, claims McLuhan,

> Wealth and work become information factors, and totally new structures are needed. . . . With electric technology, the new kinds of instant interdependence and interprocess that take over pro-duction also enter the market and social organizations. For this reason markets and education designed to cope with the products of servile toil and mechanical production are no longer adequate. Our education long ago acquired the fragmentary and piece-meal character of mechanism. It is now under increasing pressure to acquire the depth and inter-relation that are indispensable in the all-at-once world of electric organization.†

*H. M. McLuhan, *Understanding Media* (1964), p. 5.
†*Understanding Media*, p. 357.

He indicates elsewhere how the most marked expression of this pressure within the educational system is the revolutionary 'teach-in' (which reached its apotheosis in the Sorbonne debates in May).*

The confusion and mythological nature of McLuhanism, and its deeply reactionary background meaning, ought not to obscure the imaginative sensibility of many of McLuhan's insights. On the other hand, even though Adorno and his school are working within the major European tradition of social analysis deriving from Hegel and Marx, they are often astonishingly insensible to the subject-matter. In fact, both positions are right, and wrong, because neither comes to terms with the central contradiction at work in the development of such forces.

This contradiction is the reproduction on a revolutionary, world scale of the root contradiction of human society which can emerge only now from the chrysalis of material production. While society lay within this chrysalis, 'matter' dominated 'mind' and society dominated the individual. The resolution of these conflicts is only possible through the creation of the 'social individual', at the point where men begin to become capable of 'making their own history' (capable of freedom). Then, the other face of the basic sociological contradiction – the domination of society by its individual members – is released for the first time. This occurs through the development of the forces of mental production, and the formation of a 'mental surplus' whose social fate is the inverse of the material surplus hitherto decisive. Whereas the material surplus was (necessarily) appropriated by a minority, the ruling class, to free itself from drudgery and develop civilization, the mental surplus is inherently social – the most social of phenomena – and cannot be 'appropriated' in this way. It arises as the potential unity of society, the prefiguration of the classless social body, the transcendence of the split between manual and mental labour (which could only occur under the emergent dominance of the latter). However,

*The Medium is the Message (1967), pp. 100–101.

because this occurs within the historical alienation associated with the material surplus, it must struggle to exist – in the last major contradiction of history – must assume a political form, a revolutionary form, and destroy its own source.

The clearest intellectual sign of the emergence of the contradiction – before May -- was surely the growing contemporary obsession with the whole subject-matter of communication and language. While in traditional social theory this hardly counted as a problem, and there was no distinct area of study focused on it, it has now very quickly come to the forefront of sociological concern. This concern extends from the spectacular manifestation of McLuhanism, on the one hand (a general theory of history as determined by modes of communication), and the Situationist theme of '*la société du spectacle*' (modern society seen as already mainly devoted to the production of 'scenes', appearances rather than things), to the abstruse theories of French structuralism, on the other. A large sector of American sociological theory is also oriented in this direction. Marxism, naturally, has remained aloof from the intellectual harbingers of the real revolution, in comfortable contemplation of the past (identifying the mythical aspects of such novelties – signs of their deep social significance – with sad deviations from the truths of historical materialism).

It is not possible here to consider in greater detail the functioning of the contradiction. But plainly, its operation is concentrated – and felt most urgently – in the expanding workshops of mental production. Although it is a general social contradiction certain ultimately to embrace the whole social body, it is natural that it should be focused in 'higher education' and (initially) spread in shock-waves from this centre, awakening every latent contradiction of society.

There have been attempts to give some formulation to the problem already. Thus, the Professor of Sociology at Nanterre University asked (two months before the May uprising):

Today, is it possible to avoid any longer posing this question: are these student movements, from Berlin to Nanterre, from Prague to

Trento, the avant-garde signs of a new contestation of society in both theory and practice, revealing new forms of domination and new social conflicts? If it is true that knowledge and technological progress are the motors of the new society, as capital accumulation was of the old, then does not the university now occupy the same place in society as the great capitalist business once did, and does not the student movement have the same significance as the workers' movement of the previous epoch?*

This parallelism between student movements and working-class movements has also been developed more thoroughly by two American writers in a study called *Youth as a Class*. They argue that –

. . . the new proletariat is (1) the masses of the backward countries; and (2) the young of the United States.

This new 'internal proletariat' has grown up because –

The American economy is increasingly dominated by two industries that are large, public, and rapidly growing – defense and education . . . (hence) . . . the essential exploited class for the perpetuation of the existing economic system is now the young. The youth occupy the critical workplaces: they man the war-machine and the idea-factories.†

Previously, 'youth' was the biological period for the formation of the bourgeois-individualistic personality. The name of the prolonged repressive limbo which did the moulding was 'adolescence'. But the whole evolution of capitalism has made this process otiose: society no

*A. Touraine, *Naissance d'un Mouvement Étudiant*, in *Le Monde* (7th–13th March, 1968).
†J. and M. Rowntree, in the *International Socialist Journal*, No. 25 (February 1968).

longer requires entrepreneurial personalities, however it may cling to
the folklore of the heroic age of the bourgeoisie. The increasingly social
character of production demands, instead, 'organization men'. At this
point the gap between generations endemic to bourgeois society
becomes catastrophic, for the new generation is much more instinctively social than its predecessors (following the erosion of the
traditional repressive mechanisms), and this sociality encounters both
the fossils of the bourgeois *ancien régime* (parents and teachers) and
the new forms of alienation (harsher rhythms of work in higher education, a machine-like preparation for a circumscribed role in a big
organization, etc.) Caught between two forms of authoritarianism, this
'cool' (social) generation is also the focus of the most sensible and
dramatic developments of the forces of mental production:

> Youth culture can be seen as becoming increasingly collective and
> activist in the last decade . . . forms of collective activity are more
> frequent and more comprehensive, and, most importantly, modes
> of communication have become much more intensive and sophis-
> ticated. . . . Viewed in one way, 'youth culture' is an invention of
> merchandisers and a vehicle of false consciousness. However, it
> can *also* be the crucial support for alienated youth, making it pos-
> sible to translate disaffection into open revolt.*

These are the social conditions under which 'youth' can for the first
time assume an other than biological meaning, a positive social meaning as the bearer of those pressures in the social body which prefigure
a new society instead of the reproduction of the old one. When de
Gaulle spoke with condescension of 'the new blood of France', to be
'given a voice' after May, he revealed only his own ignorance of a generation which spewed out *that* 'France' along with the priests,
professors and policemen, and adopted 'Nous sommes tous des Juifs-
Allemands' as its motto, doing more for the cause of internationalism

*J. and M. Rowntree, op. cit.

and European unity in one day of May than the governments and labour bureaucracies of Western Europe had achieved in twenty years.

The analogy suggested by Touraine and the Rowntrees between the factory yesterday and the university today is interesting, as an approach to the problem. However, it is really only a metaphor, which may tend to hide the essential novelties in the present situation. The contradictions at work in it are qualitatively different from the old ones, and it is ultimately much more important to see why the university is *not* what the factory once was, why students are *not* a later generation of alienated workers (but precisely the antithesis of this, revolutionary because they negate alienation), and why youth is *not* another 'class' fitting into a conventional analysis of the social structure.

Where such radical novelties have already come into existence, and a new world has uttered its first cries, theory has to be very audacious merely to catch up with practice.

JULY 1968, HORNSEY
COLLEGE OF ART, LONDON,
*in the sixth week
of the student occupation,
in a classroom where I was
once paid to explain this
century to those too young
to understand it.*

afterword

At the end of another May, ninety-seven years ago, refugees fled across the fields north of Paris from the defeat of another revolution. Turning to look back, they saw with horror that the night sky had turned a livid red, as the Commune burned down the heart of the city rather than restore it intact into the hands of law and order.

No one could know then that the next day's ashes were to be those of European revolution itself, for almost a century. The Paris Commune of 1871 was the last of the 'old' French revolutions, the last Jacobin revolution, the last libertarian revolt of the *menu peuple*. After it, capitalism took possession of France and the earth.

May 1968 was the first 'new' French revolution, the sign that this possession is ending even at its source. Capitalism survived all the material contradictions of its history, all wars, crises, and class-struggles, and mastered the 'inevitabilities' that would destroy it again and again.

Paradoxically, real inevitability has emerged only after the material century of its triumph, in the final product of its machines: the new society alive within it, invisible yesterday, visible everywhere today, the young negation of its nature.

The anarchism of 1871 looked backwards to a pre-capitalist past, doomed to defeat; the anarchism of 1968 looks forward to the future society almost within our grasp, certain of success.

9 781859 842904

Printed in the United States
by Baker & Taylor Publisher Services